# Sincerely Yours,
# PAUL

# Sincerely Yours,

# PAUL

## 124 Sunday Readings From St. Paul, With Commentary, Arranged According to Topic

## By Leonard Foley, O.F.M.

*Nihil Obstat*
 Rev. Hilarion Kistner, O.F.M.

*Imprimi Potest:*
 Rev. Andrew Fox, O.F.M.
 Provincial

*Imprimatur:*
 +Daniel E. Pilarczyk, V.G.
 Archdiocese of Cincinnati
 December 9, 1976

Cover design and illustrations by Kieran Quinn

SBN 0-912228-35-0

# Contents

How to Use This Book . . . . . . . . . . .   xii

I. **God Our Loving Father**
   1. God's Eternal Plan . . . . . . . . .   2
   2. The Plan Carried Out in Christ . . . .   3
   3. We Are Sealed by the Spirit . . . . . .   4
   4. The Holy Trinity, God With Us . . . .   5
   5. God's Limitless Love for Us . . . . .   6
   6. How God Saves Us . . . . . . . .   7
   7. Salvation Is Entirely God's Initiative . .   8
   8. Our Sole Credit Is From God . . . . .   9
   9. Salvation Is a Gift . . . . . . . .   9
  10. God Saved Us When We Were Helpless . .   10
  11. God Creates Holiness "Out of Nothing" .   11
  12. Now the Power of God Is Our Strength
      in Holiness . . . . . . . . . . .   12
  13. God's Will Is Our Joy and Peace in the
      Spirit . . . . . . . . . . . . .   13

II. **Jesus the Son of God, Our Savior**
  14. The Word Was Made Flesh . . . . . .   16
  15. The Emptying of the Son of God . . .   17
  16. Jesus, Truly God and Truly Man . . . .   18
  17. Jesus, God and Man, Is First in Our Lives   19
  18. Jesus Is the New Adam . . . . . . .   20
  19. Jesus "Became Sin" That We Might
      Become the Holiness of God . . . .   22
  20. We Are Reconciled to God by Jesus'
      Death . . . . . . . . . . . . .   23

21. Jesus the Peacemaker Reconciles Us to
    Each Other . . . . . . . . . .          25
22. Jesus Rose "According to the Scriptures"    26
23. The Resurrection, Our Unshakable Hope       28
24. Jesus' Perfect Victory:
    Enthronement With the Father  . . .        29
25. Nothing Can Stop God's Saving Love for
    Us in Jesus . . . . . . . . . .          30
26. Jesus Is God's "Yes" to Us and Our "Yes"
    to God . . . . . . . . . . . .          31
27. Union With Jesus Is More Important Than
    Living or Dying . . . . . . . .          32
28. Jesus Alone Is Lord . . . . . . . .        33
29. Jesus Alone Is Our Riches . . . . . .      34
30. Paul, a Prime Example of the Saving
    Mercy of Jesus  . . . . . . . . .        35

## III. The Holy Spirit, the Gift

31. The Spirit Makes Us Children of God . .    38
32. The Spirit Is Our Assurance of God's
    Love for Us . . . . . . . . . .          39
33. The Spirit Lives in Us and Will Raise Us
    Up Forever . . . . . . . . . .          40
34. A Spirit-Filled Life . . . . . . . .       41
35. Christian Life in the Spirit—or Death in
    Sin . . . . . . . . . . . . .          42
36. All Gifts of the Spirit Are for Our Unity .  43
37. Particular Gifts of the Spirit  . . . . .   45
38. The Purpose of the Church:
    to Be an Open Letter to the World . .     46
39. The Church:
    a Community Called Together . . . .      47
40. Every Human Being Is Called to Christ's
    Body, the Church  . . . . . . . .        48
41. A Model Church . . . . . . . . . .         49
42. The Sevenfold Oneness of the Church . .    50
43. The Body of Christ: Unity and Variety .    51
44. Organizational and Charismatic Gifts . .   53
45. Unity in Christ as Sons and Daughters of
    the Father . . . . . . . . . .          54

46. Unity Based on the Humble Attitude of
     Christ . . . . . . . . . . . .     55
47. Remedy for Dissension:
     Awareness of God's Gifts and Call  . .     56
48. The Church Must Not Split Into Factions     57
49. Disunity Does Violence to God Himself .     59
50. Authorities in the Church Are Christ's
     Servants . . . . . . . . . .     60
51. Authority in the Church:
     Courageous Service . . . . . . . .     61
52. Paul's Authority . . . . . . . . .     62
53. The Church and the Jews  . . . . . .     64
54. The Jews Are God's Beloved People   . .     65
55. The Chosen People:
     a Warning to the Church . . . . . .     66

## IV. The Christian Life—
## Our Dying and Rising With Christ

### A. The Cross and Suffering

56. Suffering:  Living Out Our Baptismal
     Death and Resurrection  . . . . . .     70
57. The Crucified Christ Is Our Power and
     Wisdom  . . . . . . . . . . . .     71
58. The Cross, Our Only Hope . . . . . .     73
59. Christian Holiness Involves Suffering as
     Christ Did  . . . . . . . . . . .     74
60. Suffering Shows the Power of Christ
     in Us  . . . . . . . . . . . . .     75
61. Present Suffering Fades in the Light of
     Eternal Life . . . . . . . . . . .     77
62. Paul's Suffering and Death Are Acts of
     Worship  . . . . . . . . . . . .     78
63. God's Power and Glory Rest on Paul's
     Suffering . . . . . . . . . . . .     79

### B. Baptism, Our Rising to New Life in Christ

64. Putting On Christ in a Totally New Kind
     of Life . . . . . . . . . . . . .     81
65. Baptism Is Dying and Rising With Christ .     82

66. Baptism Expresses God's Graciousness
     in Jesus . . . . . . . . . . . . .      84
67. In Baptism Jesus Becomes Our Light . .      85
68. Forgiveness and Transformation . . . .      86
69. Newness in the Risen Christ . . . . .      87
70. We Are Children of God . . . . . . .      88
71. A New, Liberated Existence . . . . .      89
72. Baptism Is Our Public Profession of
     Faith . . . . . . . . . . . . . .      91

C. Our Rising Forever With Christ
73. Our Risen Bodies:
     What Will They Be Like? . . . . .      92
74. The Risen Christ Is the Promise That We
     Too Will Rise . . . . . . . . . .      93
75. Christ Will Transfigure Our Bodies to His
     Likeness . . . . . . . . . . . .      94
76. Our Resurrection: A Christian Hymn
     of Victory Over Death . . . . . . .      95
77. Heaven: We Shall Be With the Lord
     Unceasingly . . . . . . . . . . .      97

D. Eucharistic Worship
78. The Eucharist, Saving Sacrifice and
     Covenant . . . . . . . . . . . .      98
79. The Sacrament of Loving Unity . . . .      99
80. The Living Sacrifice of Our Selves . . .     100
81. Eternal Glory to God, Through Christ . .     101
82. All for the Glory of God . . . . . . .     102

E. Faith
83. We Come to Holiness Only by the Gift of
     Faith . . . . . . . . . . . . . .     103
84. The Response God Awakens in Our
     Hearts . . . . . . . . . . . . .     105
85. God Alone Creates Faith in Us . . . .     106
86. God Makes Us Holy by Our Gift of Faith     107
87. By Faith We Have Been Crucified With
     Christ and Now Live With Him . . .     109

88. Faith Is in Our Hearts and on Our Lips  .  110
89. We Move Confidently to Judgment
    Through Our Time of Faith  .  .  .  .  111
90. The Wisdom of Mature Christians  .  .  .  112
91. Faith, Hope, Charity—God's Gift and
    Our Response  .  .  .  .  .  .  .  .  .  113

F.  "As We Wait in Joyful Hope"

92. Now Is the Hour of Salvation  .  .  .  .  .  115
93. Alertness in Waiting for Christ .  .  .  .  .  116
94. The Coming of Christ Must Be Uppermost
    in Our Minds  .  .  .  .  .  .  .  .  117
95. Avoiding Anxiety About the Coming  .  .  118
96. Meanwhile, the Work of This Life  .  .  .  120
97. Peace and Joy:  Christ Is Always Near  .  121
98. Waiting for Christ:  Progress in Holiness  .  122
99. How Great the Harvest of Holiness
    Will Be .  .  .  .  .  .  .  .  .  .  .  .  123
100. Hope Sustains Us in the Sufferings of
    Life .  .  .  .  .  .  .  .  .  .  .  .  .  124
101. All Creation Hopes for Redemption.  .  .  125

G.  Charity

102. God's Greatest Gift Is Love .  .  .  .  .  .  126
103. Love Underlies All Commandments.  .  .  129
104. Charity Imitates the Father and Jesus
    and Pleases the Spirit  .  .  .  .  .  .  130
105. Charity Is All Things to All Men  .  .  .  .  131
106. Accepting One Another for God's Glory  .  132
107. Charity Does Not Look on Others in a
    Merely Human Way .  .  .  .  .  .  .  133
108. All Social Stigmas Give Way Before the
    Brotherhood of Christians  .  .  .  .  134
109. Freedom Is for Serving Others .  .  .  .  .  136
110. Christian Churches Should Aid Each
    Other Materially .  .  .  .  .  .  .  .  137

H.  Prayer

111. The Spirit Prays Within Our Prayer .  .  .  138

112. Confidence in God . . . . . . . . . 139
113. Instructions on Prayer . . . . . . . . 140
114. Prayer of Gratitude . . . . . . . . . 142

I. Marriage and Celibacy

115. Christian Marriage Symbolizes the Love
     of Christ and His Church . . . . . . 143
116. The Christian Family Is the Concrete
     Expression of the Church . . . . . 145
117. Celibacy as an Enabling Way of Life . . 146
118. Chastity for All Christians . . . . . . 148

J. Proclaiming the Good News

119. We Have No Choice But to Proclaim the
     Good News . . . . . . . . . . . 149
120. Apostolic Proclamation of the Good
     News . . . . . . . . . . . . . 150
121. Proclaiming the Good News Entails
     Hardship . . . . . . . . . . . . 151
122. Paul, the Authentic Apostle . . . . . . 152
123. Paul, the Selfless Missionary . . . . . 153

V. The End and the Beginning
124. Glory to God in the Highest! . . . . . 156

Indexes
Index of Sundays . . . . . . . . . . . 160
Index of Scripture References . . . . . . . 162
Index of Topics . . . . . . . . . . . . 164

## How to Use This Book

About one third of St. Paul's writings are read at Sunday and feastday Masses over a three-year period—presumably "the best of St. Paul." In these selections from his letters, we hear the "Good News of Jesus" as Paul experienced it and interpreted it to the early Christian communities.

Many of the letters deal with particular situations in the Churches: factions at Corinth, misunderstanding of the Second Coming in Thessalonia, conflict between Jewish and Gentile groups, eating meat offered to idols. But Paul always brings his readers to the vision of the glory of the Christian life.

He complements the simple statement of the Church's faith as we find it in Matthew, Mark and Luke; he balances the majestic Christ of St. John with the Lord who emptied himself to take the form of a slave.

This book attempts to capture the beauty and inspiration of St. Paul's mind and heart in a systematic arrangement of the Church's Sunday selections from his writings—a sort of catechism, to use a much maligned word. The major divisions treat of God the Father, Jesus, the Holy Spirit, the Church, the Christian Life. Any of the units can be used independently, for prayer or study.

The commentary relies heavily on two standard works: *The Jerome Biblical Commentary*, published by Prentice-Hall and the *New Catholic Commentary*, published by Nelson.

There are three indexes. The first will enable the reader to find the reading and commentary for any Sunday of the year when St. Paul is read. The second refers the reader to particular quotations from St. Paul. The third is a subject index.

The Sundays of the year are referred to by number—for example, "16" means the 16th Sunday of the year. The three-year cycle of readings is referred to as A, B, C. Thus "16C" means the 16th Sunday of the year in the C cycle. Some selections are read annually.

A few readings have been divided and the parts treated in separate chapters because of a difference in subject matter. In this case the letter "a" after the Sunday number indicates the first part of the reading. Thus "16C-a" means the first part of the reading for the 16th Sunday of the C cycle; "b" refers to the second part.

# I. God Our Loving Father

GOD CHOSE
US BEFORE
THE WORLD
BEGAN

# 1. God's Eternal Plan

Eph 1, 3-6
15B-a
2 of Christmas-a
Immaculate Conception-a

Praised be the God and Father of our Lord Jesus Christ,
who has bestowed on us in Christ
every spiritual blessing in the heavens!
God chose us in him before the world began,
to be holy and blameless in his sight,
to be full of love;
he likewise predestined us through Christ Jesus
to be his adopted sons—
such was his will and pleasure—
that all might praise the divine favor
he has bestowed on us in his beloved.

This might be called the "inside story" of creation—
what God had in mind as he made our world. From eternity he planned a Christ-community that was to include all humanity.

Our finest response is to praise the Father for the blessings he gives us. We have, Paul says, every Spirit-ual blessing, because all God's gifts are summed up in God's gift of the Spirit. We are God's children, we are forgiven, we are members of Christ's Body. We are blessed in the heavenly places, that is, "where" Christ is now glorious-ly enthroned after his death and resurrection. He is one of us. Because of our baptismal union with him, we are "there" too.

All this was eternally in God's mind. The plan to make Christ the head of a brotherhood is as "old" as God. God eternally saw all history, innocence and sin, and placed Jesus at the center of it, as savior. He was *pleased* to do this, being a gracious God. His plan was not an afterthought, but a deliberate, loving initiative.

He destined us—the community, the Body of Christ— to be holy and blameless, like the sacrifices the Jews were to offer. Our holiness is interior. In fact, *we* are

2

the offering, made pleasing by our oneness with Christ our Priest.

Why all this? That we, recognizing this beautiful eternal plan, might praise and thank God and so find our happiness. God opens himself up to us graciously. In wonder and amazement, we respond in joyful praise. Thus, life is mutual blessing: God blesses us with all he has; in Christ's Spirit, we are able to spend our lives blessing him in return.

## 2. The Plan Carried Out in Christ

Eph 1, 7-10
15B-b

It is in Christ and through his blood
that we have been redeemed
and our sins forgiven,
so immeasurably generous is God's favor to us.
God has given us the wisdom
to understand fully the mystery,
the plan he was pleased to decree in Christ,
to be carried out in the fullness of time:
namely, to bring all things
in the heavens and on earth
into one under Christ's headship.

Just as God freed his people from Egyptian slavery, so he has freed us from the slavery of sin. He has made us his own, through the blood of Christ shed on the cross. To the Jewish mind, *blood is life*. Jesus pours out his life, and it is poured into us. The pouring of blood cleansed and consecrated us. God himself came to make a cleansing-consecrating sacrifice. His coming was sheer grace, pure love, not vindictive justice.

Faith enables us to see this eternal plan now brought

3

into history by Christ. This is the fullness of time, an entirely new era not measured by clocks. Now God's full power is released through Christ. The plan was to reunite the whole universe, shattered by sin, into a community of persons in Christ.


### 3. We Are Sealed by the Spirit

Eph 1, 11-14
15B-c
Immaculate Conception-b

In him we [Jewish people] were chosen;
for in the decree of God,
who administers everything according to his will and
    counsel,
we were predestined to praise his glory
by being the first to hope in Christ.
In him you [Gentiles] too were chosen;
when you heard the glad tidings of salvation,
the word of truth,
and believed in it,
you were sealed with the Holy Spirit who had been
    promised.
He is the pledge of our inheritance,
the first payment against the full redemption
of a people God has made his own
to praise his glory.


Both Jew and Gentile—all humankind—are saved in Christ. The Jews were chosen to "pre-hope" in Christ the Messiah. The Gentiles too are now heirs, since they have been sealed with the Spirit promised by the prophets. To seal or stamp implied ownership; Baptism is the sealing of Christians.

The Spirit is the downpayment, or first installment, of full salvation. Our salvation is already achieved, but not yet fully realized: our life grows toward the coming of Christ. All this is God's will, and what he wills he effectively carries out.

Again, the purpose: that we may be filled with his life, so that our greatest happiness is to praise his glory.

These first three readings have clearly spoken of the Trinity: the plan of the Father, redemption in Christ, the seal of the Spirit.


## 4. The Holy Trinity, God With Us

2 Cor 13, 11-13
Trinity A

Brothers, mend your ways.
Encourage one another.
Live in harmony and peace,
and the God of love and peace will be with you.
Greet one another with a holy kiss.
All the holy ones send greetings to you.
The grace of the Lord Jesus Christ,
and the love of God,
and the fellowship of the Holy Spirit
be with you all!

Paul concludes his letter to the Church of Corinth by encouraging them to have the qualities of a true Christian community. His final blessing, which expressly mentions the Holy Trinity, is now used at the beginning of Mass.

He prays that the people of Corinth may have, first, the *grace of Christ*. The word for grace is *charis*, which means "love" (charity) and "gift" (charism). Christ is mentioned first because he is our visible way to God, the revelation of the grace of God. Paul asks that they may have the *love of God—agape*, the selfless, overflowing love God has for us. It is a fatherly love, eager to adopt us as children; a steadfast covenant love. Third, he asks for *the fellowship of the Holy Spirit*, that is, the communication by the Holy Spirit of the fullness of God's love. The Spirit is the life-principle within us, our communion with God, our holiness.

This loving God wants only the good of the people of Corinth. Therefore they should "mend their ways." The Greek expression suggests the straightening out of something that has been bent out of shape. They are to stand beside one another as "paracletes"—aides and encouragers, like the Spirit.

## 5. God's Limitless Love for Us

Rom 8, 31-34
2 Lent B

If God is for us, who can be against us?
Is it possible that he who did not spare his own Son
but handed him over for the sake of us all
will not grant us all things besides?
Who shall bring a charge against God's chosen ones?
God, who justifies?
Who shall condemn them?
Christ Jesus, who died or rather was raised up,
who is at the right hand of God
and who intercedes for us?

All problems, doubts and sufferings fade into insignificance when we consider God's love for us. This is the basis for unshakable Christian confidence. We can only marvel at the unfathomable goodness of the God who is "on our side."

There is a suggestion of a law-court situation in which someone would demand a verdict of "guilty" for us. But no prosecutor is to be found. The rhetorical questions imply negative answers. No one will condemn us.

Our confidence is based, first of all, on the great gift God has given us in his Son. If he would give the Greatest Gift, what else can he possibly refuse? We can only guess what it "cost" God to see his Son suffer.

Our confidence rests on the fact that God is one who "justifies," makes holy—not the one who condemns. We are his chosen, not his rejected, people.

Finally, we have confidence because of Christ who is raised to the right hand of God, the propitious place. He continues his saving work praying to the Father for us.

## 6. How God Saves Us

Rom 8, 28-30
17A

We know that God makes all things work together
for the good of those who love him,
who have been called according to his decree.
Those whom he foreknew he predestined
to share the image of his Son,
that the Son might be the first born of many brothers.
Those he predestined he likewise called;
those he called he also justified;
and those he justified he in turn glorified.

There is no limit to God's love. Whether we recognize it or not, it is behind everything that happens.

Though his eternal plan is carried out in steps, it is all one in God's mind. Four steps call for a fifth: 1) He foreknew us; 2) He eternally destined us to be his children; 3) He called us; 4) He justified us, that is, made us holy, transforming us to be like Jesus; 5) He will complete what he has begun: he will glorify us.

7

All this happens to those who love God in response. Their glory is that they can be actual brothers and sisters of the elder brother, Jesus, the firstborn of the new family of God.

## 7. Salvation Is Entirely God's Initiative

2 Tm 1, 8-10
2 Lent A

Bear your share of the hardship
which the gospel entails.
God has saved us and has called us to a holy life,
not because of any merit of ours
but according to his own design—
the grace held out to us in Christ Jesus
before the world began
but now made manifest through the appearance of our
    Savior.
He has robbed death of its power
and has brought life and immortality
into clear light through the gospel.

We easily fall into the error of thinking we can save ourselves by our good efforts to be holy. One of Paul's persistent emphases is that only God can save us, free us from slavery, give us his life. Salvation is grace, that is, it is freely, gratuitously given, simply because of God's infinite love, independently of our merit.

This eternal plan came to light when Jesus was born. He robbed death of its power, gave us life, indeed eternal life. This is the same as saying that the purpose of the plan was to give us holiness—the gift of being one with Christ in a divinely-powered life of love for the Father and each other.

## 8. Our Sole Credit Is From God

2 Cor 3, 4-6
8B-b

This great confidence in God is ours, through Christ.
It is not that we are entitled of ourselves
to take credit for anything.
Our sole credit is from God,
who has made us qualified ministers of a new covenant,
a covenant not of a written law but of spirit.
The written law kills, but the Spirit gives life.

"Our sole credit is from God" refers primarily to the power of the apostles, including Paul; implicitly it refers to all holy actions. The Second Council of Orange cited this verse against heretics and insisted that God's grace is essential even for the initial act of faith.

The Mosaic Law "killed" because it commanded without enabling. The New Covenant is not limited to a written code (e.g., the Ten Commandments, which can remain external observances); the Spirit imposes his commandments within us.

## 9. Salvation Is a Gift

Col 1, 12-14
34C-a

Give thanks to the Father
for having made you worthy
to share the lot of the saints in light.
He rescued us from the power of darkness
and brought us into the kingdom of his beloved Son.
Through him we have redemption,
the forgiveness of our sins.

We are now the Lord's own inheritance or "lot"—

something he treasures, just as the Chosen People trea-
sured the land he gave them as their inheritance. We
have been redeemed and forgiven just as they were
rescued from slavery in Egypt.

We are fellow-citizens of the saints, made worthy
with them to be members of the Kingdom.

### 10. God Saved Us When We Were Helpless

Eph 2, 4-10
4 Lent B

God is rich in mercy;
because of his great love for us
he brought us to life with Christ
when we were dead in sin.
By this favor you were saved.
Both with and in Christ Jesus
he raised us up and gave us a place in the heavens,
that in the ages to come
he might display the great wealth of his favor,
manifested by his kindness to us in Christ Jesus.
I repeat, it is owing to his favor that salvation is yours
        through faith.
This is not your own doing, it is God's gift;
neither is it a reward for anything you have
        accomplished,
so let no one pride himself on it.
We are truly his handiwork, created in Christ Jesus
to lead the life of good deeds which God prepared for
        us in advance.

Even if we were totally innocent, we would be totally
dependent on God. But the wonder of God's grace is
that he loved us and saved us even when we were sinners.

"Sinners" refers to the human race as such, for all are
included in God's plan. But we can take it as a reference

to God's unceasing love for us even now in our personal sinfulness. He is always the Father seeking the Prodigal Son.

God comes to us through Christ. He is the center of creation. All things find meaning in him. Paul emphasizes our "with-ness"—we are com-panions, co-sharers, co-heirs. Our Baptism parallels Jesus' dying and rising to glory. We are created in him not only in our being but in our activity—which is less our action than God's action in us through Christ. Our role is to respond to that action, to do the good things God "prepared for us in advance." His power always waits to be accepted by our freedom.

## 11. God Creates Holiness 'Out of Nothing'

1 Cor 1, 26-31
4A

Brothers, you are among those called.
Consider your own situation.
Not many of you are wise, as men account wisdom;
not many are influential;
and surely not many are wellborn.
God chose those whom the world considers absurd to
     shame the wise;
he singled out the weak of this world to shame the
     strong.
He chose the world's lowborn and despised,
those who count for nothing,
to reduce to nothing those who were something;
so that mankind can do no boasting before God.
God it is who has given you life in Christ Jesus.
He has made him our wisdom and also our justice,
our sanctification, and our redemption.
This is just as you find it written,
"Let him who would boast, boast in the Lord."

11

Each of the factions in the Church of Corinth thought itself better than the others. Paul uses this unfortunate human weakness to remind them of a basic fact: even if God's choice had depended on human worth, *they* would not be among the chosen ones. Few of them are "high society"; they have little "clout" in Corinth, being of a lower class; and they have little wisdom and education.

In fact, God chose them, rather than those whom the world would consider likely choices, precisely to show that only divine power can give divine life, holiness.

God takes us and transforms us "out of nothing," as it were, into holy persons. So, if there is to be any boasting, it must be done in Christ. He alone is the source of our value.

### 12. Now the Power of God Is Our Strength in Holiness

Phil 4, 12-14.19-20
28A

I am experienced in being brought low,
yet I know what it is to have an abundance.
I have learned how to cope with every circumstance—
how to eat well or go hungry,
to be well provided for or do without.
In him who is the source of my strength
I have strength for everything.
Nonetheless, it was kind of you
to want to share in my hardships.
My God in turn will supply your needs fully,
in a way worthy of his magnificent riches in Christ
     Jesus.
All glory to our God and Father
for unending ages! Amen.

Paul says three times that he has come to appreciate the extremes of wealth and poverty—the not-having-enough and the having-more-than-enough. Now he knows that it is God who enables him to resist the temptations that go with wealth and the equally dangerous problems of being poor.

Rather he has reached a new kind of strength: literally, "I am able *every which way* in the one empowering me."

He has accepted so deep a consciousness of God's possessing love that he is relatively indifferent to anything else—pain or pleasure, success or failure.

## 13. God's Will Is Our Joy and Peace in the Spirit

1 Thes 5, 16-24
3 Advent B

Rejoice always, never cease praying, render constant
     thanks;
such is God's will for you in Christ Jesus.
Do not stifle the spirit.
Do not despise prophecies.
Test everything; retain what is good.
Avoid any semblance of evil.
May the God of peace make you perfect in holiness.
May you be preserved whole and entire, spirit, soul, and
     body,
irreproachable at the coming of our Lord Jesus Christ.
He who calls us is trustworthy,
therefore he will do it.

Christianity is a way of life that embraces charity, joy, thanks and constant prayer. If only we could take Paul's word that it is *these* things that are "God's will," not the cold and mechanical, eternally-typed-out list of directions we have sometimes mistaken for it.

13

God's will is that we open ourselves to his self-revealing and discern his call here and now as clearly as possible. God's will is our conscientious decision, informed by all he has told us and by his living Spirit within us. On the one hand, we must not *quench* this Spirit by a narrow and rigid concept of God's will, which is endlessly creative, beyond all imagining. Yet, our conscience must also *test* everything by the full revelation the Spirit has given us.

This activity, Paul always insists, swims in the ocean of joyful and grateful prayer. A peaceful God is bringing us—whole persons with body and soul inextricably joined—to the fullness of holiness. He is the one who is making us ready for the joy of meeting Jesus. He began the process; he may be trusted to complete it.

# II. Jesus the Son of God, Our Savior

## 14. The Word Was Made Flesh

Ti 2, 11-14
Christmas Midnight

The grace of God has appeared,
offering salvation to all men.
It trains us to reject godless ways and worldly desires,
and live temperately, justly and devoutly in this age
as we await our blessed hope,
the appearing of the glory of the great God
and of our Savior Christ Jesus.
It was he who sacrificed himself for us,
to redeem us from all unrighteousness
and to cleanse for himself a people of his own,
eager to do what is right.

God's freely-given love—his graciousness beyond all
demands of faithfulness—became *visible*. Jesus is the
sacrament or outward sign of God, the final perfect
revelation. He is both our "great God" and our Savior,
making a gift (grace) of himself.

Our new life is contrasted with the life of sin. Just as
God purified the Israelites and made a covenant with
them, so Jesus chose and purified the people of the New
Covenant.

Since we belong to God, we are made holy and are
called to be holy. God himself trains us in the new life
so that we will be inspired and eager to do good works.
The ideal Christian life is here expressed from a Greek
viewpoint: it is one of moderation, self-discipline,
devoutness, piety as we wait for the second visible coming of our Savior.

## 15. The Emptying of the Son of God

Phil 2, 6-11
Passion Sunday
26A-b

Your attitude must be Christ's:

Though he was in the form of God,
   he did not deem equality with God
   something to be grasped at.

Rather, he emptied himself
   and took the form of a slave,
   being born in the likeness of men.

He was known to be of human estate,
   and it was thus that he humbled himself,
   obediently accepting even death,
   death on a cross!

Because of this,
   God highly exalted him
   and bestowed on him the name
   above every other name,

So that at Jesus' name
   every knee must bend
   in the heavens, on the earth,
   and under the earth,
   and every tongue proclaim
   to the glory of God the Father:
   JESUS CHRIST IS LORD!

At Philippi, members of the Church could not give up their "rivalry and conceit." Paul reminds them of the great "emptying" of the Son of God, who for our sakes was willing to give up the glory due him as God. He could stand having his divinity concealed, his authority "lost." The Son emptied himself and took a human nature in order to share the human plight. He let himself be enslaved, like his brothers and sisters, to the

17

powers of evil, to death, to everything but sin. Even more than that, he let his death be a degrading one, that of a criminal.

Because of this total loving obedience to the Father in death, he was raised from the lowest humiliation to the highest glory. Now, as God-man (not only as the Eternal Son), he receives the name of Lord, Yahweh, and deserves the adoration of the universe.

If God could let go his claim to divinity, Paul said, then you people of Philippi can surely let go of your rivalries and conceits.

### 16. Jesus, Truly God and Truly Man

Rom 1, 1-7
4 Advent A

Greetings from Paul, a servant of Christ Jesus,
called to be an apostle and set apart to proclaim the
    gospel of God
which he promised long ago through his prophets,
as the holy Scriptures record—
the gospel concerning his Son,
who was descended from David according to the flesh
but was made Son of God in power,
according to the spirit of holiness,
by his resurrection from the dead:
Jesus Christ our Lord.
Through him we have been favored with apostleship,
that we may spread his name
and bring to obedient faith all the Gentiles,
among whom are you who have been called
to belong to Jesus Christ.
To all in Rome, beloved of God and called to holiness,
grace and peace from God our Father
and the Lord Jesus Christ.

The Good News of God is *Jesus*—God emptying himself to take human nature on himself, so that we could take God's life into our own lives by the mystery of grace.

Jesus is man and God, God-man. He is eternally the Son of God, and yet he was "made" Son of God in power when the Father raised Jesus out of death to the glory of resurrection. Jesus as *God-man* now has power to send his Spirit to save the world.

Jesus is God and *man*. He was a Jew, descended from David in the flesh, human in all things as we are, except for sin. He knows what it is to feel, to be faced with decisions, to trust, to fear, to be hurt, to laugh, to love and be loved, to succeed and fail—and to die.

Once possessed by this Good News, we spread his name by our lives. God calls all human beings to his holiness—the gift of life in Jesus—and we are his voice of invitation.

## 17. Jesus, God and Man, Is First in Our Lives

Col 1, 15-20
15C
34C-b

He is the image of the invisible God,
the firstborn of all creatures.
In him everything in heaven and on earth was created,
things visible and invisible,
whether thrones or dominations, principalities or
     powers;
all were created through him, and for him.
He is before all else that is.
In him everything continues in being.
It is he who is head of the body, the Church;
he who is the beginning, the firstborn of the dead,

so that primacy may be his in everything.
It pleased God to make absolute fullness
reside in him and, by means of him,
to reconcile everything in his person,
everything, I say,
both on earth and in the heavens,
making peace through the blood of his cross.

Paul speaks of the absolute first-ness of Jesus. He is
the image of God as Wisdom-made-flesh. He is also the
perfect image of God as man (unlike Adam, who spoiled
his image). He is the visible and radiant appearance of
God. He is the firstborn of many brothers and sisters
who form his Body; they depend on him and are
modeled after him.

A new creation began in him. Yet all creation, before
and after his birth, depends on him. He is the first one
born of the dead, that is, by his resurrection; because of
it, we will rise again with him.

Finally, he is the fullness of God: All that is in God
is in him, and he fills the Church with fullness of life
and love.

## 18. Jesus Is the New Adam

Rom 5, 12-15, 17-19
1 Lent A
12A

Through one man sin entered the world
and with sin death,
death thus coming to all men inasmuch as all sinned—
before the law there was sin in the world,
even though sin is not imputed when there is no law—
I say, from Adam to Moses death reigned,
even over those who had not sinned by breaking a
        precept as did Adam,

that type of the Man to come.
But the gift is not like the offense.
For if by the offense of the one man all died,
much more did the grace of God
and the gracious gift of the one man, Jesus Christ,
   abound for all.
If death began its reign through one man because of
   his offense,
much more shall those who receive the overflowing
   grace and gift of justice
live and reign through the one man, Jesus Christ.
To sum up, then:
just as a single offense brought condemnation to all
   men,
a single righteous act brought all men acquittal and
   life.
Just as through one man's disobedience all became
   sinners,
so through one man's obedience all shall become just.


Paul contrasts Adam, the originator of sin, with Jesus, the originator of redemption.

The image is that of a court case. Adam, a guilty defendant, was sentenced to death and lost our inheritance. Jesus, an innocent victim, received not a sentence (though he seemed to), but rather the gift of redeeming all humankind and giving them an eternal inheritance.

But Paul's main point here is to extol the *superabundance* of Christ's grace. Adam's sin affected all humankind; so does Christ's redemption. But it is far in excess of any "normal" forgiveness we might possibly have hoped for.

Our connection with Adam is the explanation of the presence of evil in the world. Paul sees sin as a personified evil force which has taken possession of humanity. Real sin, of course, is personal. Sin produces its full effect of eternal death through one's personal sin, which ratifies Adam's voluntary separation from God.

So also, our connection with Christ is the explana-

tion of all the good we have. Christ's saving death and
resurrection joins us again to God. It produces its full
effect of eternal life through our personal ratification
of his reconciling us to God—by our faith and love.

### 19. Jesus 'Became Sin'
### That We Might Become the Holiness of God

2 Cor 5, 17-21
4 Lent C

If anyone is in Christ, he is a new creation.
The old order has passed away; now all is new!
All this has been done by God,
who has reconciled us to himself through Christ
and has given us the ministry of reconciliation.
I mean that God, in Christ, was reconciling the world
     to himself,
not counting men's transgressions against them,
and that he has entrusted the message of reconciliation
     to us.
This makes us ambassadors for Christ,
God as it were appealing through us.
We implore you, in Christ's name:
be reconciled to God!
For our sakes
God made him who did not know sin to be sin,
so that in him we might become the very holiness
     of God.

God himself took the initiative of reconciliation, even
though he was the one offended. He does not "reckon
our offenses"; in Christ he appeals to the human race as
if no one had ever sinned.

This is the heart of the matter: Christ was made
"sin" that we might become the holiness of God. Jesus
did not know sin by personal experience. Yet, in some

way God in Christ took on himself the sin of the world.
Christ identified himself with us in our sin. He became
so involved in us that he shared our misery, the results
of sin. God chose to be, as it were, the carrier of sin and
to be identified with its evil effects.

Love was bound to suffer as though it were as sinful
as the beloved, so as to set man right with God.

Scripture says: "The Lord laid upon him the guilt of
us all. . . .A grave was assigned him among the wicked
and a burial place with evildoers" (Is 53, 6. 9). "Christ
delivered us from the power of the law's curse by himself becoming a curse for us" (Gal 3, 13). "God sent his
Son in the likeness of sinful flesh as a sin offering, thereby condemning sin in the flesh" (Rom 8, 3).

Probably "sin" here means "sin offering." In the Old
Testament, the word meant sin, the results of sin, and
the offering for sin. The sacrifice looked to the reestab-
lishment of the covenant relationship between God and
man destroyed by sin. By the outpouring of *blood*
(which was *life*, the divine element in man), life was
released, poured out upon us, so that we become a
new creation.

Because of his solidarity with us (which of course we
are called to accept voluntarily), our sin was killed when
he was killed, so that the saving mercy (justice) of God
might be communicated to us.

We are changed in the depths of our being. We are
essentially different from what we were before. We
"become the goodness of God."

## 20. We Are Reconciled to God by Jesus' Death

Rom 5, 6-11
11A

At the appointed time,
when we were still powerless,

Christ died for us godless men.
It is rare that anyone should lay down his life for a
    just man,
though it is barely possible that for a good man
someone may have the courage to die.
It is precisely in this
that God proves his love for us:
that while we were still sinners, Christ died for us.
Now that we have been justified by his blood,
it is all the more certain
that we shall be saved by him from God's wrath.
For if, when we were God's enemies,
we were reconciled to him by the death of his Son,
it is all the more certain
that we who have been reconciled
will be saved by his life.
Not only that;
we go so far as to make God our boast
through our Lord Jesus Christ,
through whom we have now received reconciliation.

We find it hard to believe that the sinner is *incapable* of doing anything to achieve his rightness with God. Forgiveness is always God's initiative of love. He saves us by the death and resurrection of his Son. He loves us even when we are sinners, and eternally sees us redeemed in the blood of Christ.

Now that we have received the gift of his friendship, by responding in faith to his love, how much more can we expect final salvation, since Christ is risen and with the Father. We *have been* reconciled by Jesus' death, and we *will be* saved by his risen life. This is *one* event, not two. The death-resurrection of Jesus, taken together, is our one salvation. But it involves an "already" and a "not yet" for us. We have already been "justified," made holy (the beginning of salvation), and we can be confident that we will be saved (final salvation).

How far God's love is above man's love! We would not give up our lives, ordinarily, for another human being. Well, possibly for a really good person. But Christ died for us when we were sinners. He loves us no matter what we do. God is always there for us, no matter how we fail to respond. He is always waiting.

Instead of being terrified of God, we can now "boast"—that is, *exult* in the very thought of God and *glory* in the love he has given us.


21.  Jesus the Peacemaker Reconciles Us to Each Other

Eph 2, 13-18
16B

In Christ Jesus you who once were far off
have been brought near
through the blood of Christ.
It is he who is our peace,
and who made the two of us one
by breaking down the barrier of hostility
that kept us apart.
In his own flesh he abolished the law
with its commands and precepts,
to create in himself one new man
from us who had been two
and to make peace,
reconciling both of us to God
in one body
through his cross
which put that enmity to death.
He came and "announced the good news of peace
to you who were far off,
and to those who were near";
through him we both have access in one Spirit
to the Father.


Jesus' death broke down the barrier between Jew and Gentile—and every other division among persons. Now there is only one Body—the Church, the Body of Christ.

He abolished the Law insofar as it was a source of division between Jew and Gentile, giving mankind a far more inclusive command—to love as he did.

Gentiles did not become Jews; neither side "gave in." Rather, all divisions are transformed into one new humanity, the Body of Christ. The way to this new humanity is Jesus' cross.

## 22. Jesus Rose 'According to the Scriptures'

1 Cor 15, 1-11
5C

Brothers, I want to remind you
of the gospel I preached to you,
which you received and in which you stand firm.
You are being saved by it at this very moment
if you retain it as I preached it to you.
Otherwise you have believed in vain.
I handed on to you, first of all,
what I myself received,
that Christ died for our sins
in accord with the Scriptures;
that he was buried
and, in accord with the Scriptures,
rose on the third day;
that he was seen by Cephas, then by the Twelve.
After that he was seen
by five hundred brothers at once,
most of whom are still alive,
although some have fallen asleep.
Next he was seen by James; then by all the apostles.
Last of all he was seen by me,
as one born out of the normal course.
I am the least of the apostles;
in fact, because I persecuted the church of God,
I do not even deserve the name.

But by God's favor I am what I am.
This favor of his to me
has not proved fruitless.
Indeed, I have worked harder than all the others,
not on my own but through the favor of God.
In any case, whether it be I or they,
this is what we preach
and this is what you believed.

The resurrection is a historical fact, attested by witnesses. This was the tradition already existing in the Church before it was received by Paul. Now he adds his own witness, almost certainly referring to his experience on the road to Damascus.

The Good News whereby they *are being* saved is that Jesus died and rose, according to the Scriptures.

The first preaching stressed that Jesus' death and resurrection was "according to the Scriptures," that is, it fulfilled their whole promise. Specifically, Paul was probably referring to the famous Servant passages: Isaiah 52, 13—53, 12; Psalm 16, 10 (". . .You will not abandon my soul to the nether world, nor will you suffer your faithful one to undergo corruption. You will show me the path to life, fullness of joys in your presence, the delights at your right hand forever"); Hosea 6, 1 ("Come, let us return to the Lord, for it is he who has rent, but he will heal us; he has struck us, but he will bind our wounds. He will revive us after two days; on the third day he will raise us up, to live in his presence"); and Jonah 2, 1.

Paul first cites the official witnesses—Peter and the Twelve; then 500 Christians; then James; and finally himself. He is one of the official witnesses, but he appears suddenly among them, "like one born out of the normal course." This can also mean "monster" in Greek. He may be quoting an insult thrown at him.

Note Paul's combining of grace and works: "I have worked harder. . .not on my own but by the grace of God."

### 23. The Resurrection, Our Unshakable Hope

1 Cor 15, 20-26.28
34A,
Assumption

Christ has been raised from the dead,
the first fruits of those who have fallen asleep.
Death came through a man;
hence the resurrection of the dead
comes through a man also.
Just as in Adam all die,
so in Christ all will come to life again,
but each one in proper order:
Christ the first-fruits and then, at his coming,
all those who belong to him.
After that will come the end,
when after having destroyed every sovereignty,
      authority, and power,
he will hand over the kingdom to God the Father.
Christ must reign
until God has put all enemies under his feet,
and the last enemy to be destroyed is death.
When, finally, all has been subjected to the Son,
he will then subject himself
to the One who made all things subject to him,
so that God may be all in all.

Jesus' resurrection to a new and glorious life is the fruit of his death on the cross. Together, his death and resurrection are our salvation. Death—physical and moral—is turned into new physical and spiritual, eternal life in Jesus. He is the first one to be reborn from the dead, the first of many who will share his victory.

The liturgical offering of "first fruits" implied the consecration of the whole harvest. So the offering of Jesus, the "first fruits" of humanity, implies God's plan to bring all mankind to himself.

Adam's sin brought spiritual death, of which physical death is a sign. The voluntary, loving, physical death of Christ resulted in new divine life for us; our bodily resurrection will be the fruit of that life.

Our resurrection will occur at Christ's coming. (Paul speaks here only of the resurrection of the just.)

In the meantime, we are in process—while Christ gains mastery over all the forces hostile to his Father's "field," the world. At the end, Christ will hand over his kingdom—the mastered world, the entire harvest—to his Father.

### 24. Jesus' Perfect Victory: Enthronement With the Father

Eph 1, 20-23
Ascension-b

[God's power in us] is like the strength he showed
in raising Christ from the dead
and seating him at his right hand in heaven,
high above every principality, power, virtue and
    domination,
and every name that can be given
in this age or the age to come.
He has put all things under Christ's feet
and has made him thus exalted,
head of the church, which is his body:
the fullness of him
who fills the universe in all its parts.

The Father's eternal plan now reaches its glorious, perfect fulfillment. The life-death-resurrection cycle ends with Jesus raised as God-man to full equality with the Father. He is now able to save the whole world. He has supremacy over all creation. All other "powers" on earth, good and bad, are now subject to him. When he was on earth they seemed able to destroy him. Now there is nothing that can stop the saving love of God.

Divine power pours out through him into his Body,

the Church, his visible community on earth. The Church manifests the love of God for the world and exercises his power to save. The Father's power which raised Christ is now available to us. Individually and as a Body, we are being "filled up" to be a sign of Christ's love. God's power flows into the Church, makes it grow, produces the good lives of Christians. The redemption has been achieved once and for all, but this "filling up" with Christ goes on to the end of time.

## 25. Nothing Can Stop God's Saving Love for Us in Jesus

Rom 8, 35.37-39
18A

Who will separate us from the love of Christ?
Trial, or distress, or persecution, or hunger,
or nakedness, or danger, or the sword?
Yet in all this we are more than conquerors
because of him who has loved us.
For I am certain that neither death nor life,
neither angels nor principalities,
neither the present nor the future,
nor powers,
neither height nor depth
nor any other creature,
will be able to separate us from the love of God
that comes to us in Christ Jesus, our Lord.

God's love for us in Christ is absolutely certain. Nothing can stop it. And nothing can destroy our love for Christ. None of the dangers and troubles of life can make us forget the love of Christ made known to us in his death and resurrection.

The thought of Christ's unfailing love for us fills Paul

with confidence. Triumphantly he celebrates this love—
whose greatest work is to maintain a love for God in us,
strong enough to make us triumph over every obstacle
and to support us in every suffering. Paul goes through
all the various "powers" considered hostile to man. It is
absolutely certain that none of them has the power to
check or weaken God's love for us which is always at
work through Christ Jesus.

## 26.  Jesus Is God's 'Yes' to Us and Our 'Yes' to God

2 Cor 1, 18-22
7B

As God keeps his word,
I declare that my word to you
is not "yes" one minute and "no" the next.
Jesus Christ,
whom Silvanus, Timothy, and I
preached to you as Son of God,
was not alternately "yes" and "no";
he was never anything but "yes."
Whatever promises God has made
have been fulfilled in him;
therefore it is through him
that we address our Amen to God
when we worship together.
God is the one who firmly establishes us
along with you in Christ;
it is he who anointed us and has sealed us,
thereby depositing the first payment,
the Spirit in our hearts.

Paul changed his plan to revisit the Corinthians, and
was thereupon accused of being fickle. He makes a bold
answer, which goes far beyond the particular problem:
God's own faithfulness is the guarantee of Paul's, be-

cause he has absorbed the Spirit of Christ.

Christ is *the* faithful one. He is always "Yes," that is, he is God's "Yes, I will!" to all human hopes. Jesus is the Yes of the Father, keeping all his promises, bringing them to fulfillment.

Jesus becomes our Yes in the liturgy: We say our Amen (or Yes) to God with perfect confidence through Christ.

Returning to the notion of stability, Paul repeats that God has given his own trustworthiness to the apostles and all the faithful by uniting them to Christ, the expression of his own fidelity. This communion with Christ is realized by three baptismal gifts: we are anointed, once and for all, in full consecration; we are sealed by the "stamp" of God, as owners put a stamp on their property; and we have the Spirit as a pledge, or down payment, on God's final and perfect fulfillment of his promises.

### 27. Union With Jesus Is More Important Than Living or Dying

Phil 1, 20-24.27
25A

Christ will be exalted through me,
whether I live or die.
For, to me, "life" means Christ;
hence dying is so much gain.
If, on the other hand,
I am to go on living in the flesh,
that means productive toil for me—
and I do not know which to prefer.
I am strongly attracted by both:
I long to be freed from this life
and to be with Christ,
for that is the far better thing;

32

yet it is more urgent
that I remain alive for your sakes.
Conduct yourselves, then,
in a way worthy of the gospel of Christ.

Paul is in prison, possibly facing death. He meditates
on what his death may mean. Living, whether in heaven
or on earth, is union with Christ, or it is not life. It does
not really matter whether he lives or dies, since Christ
will be honored in either case. The glory of Christ, after
all, is more important to Paul than his own life or death.

Christ is the beginning, end and inspiration of his
whole life. To live on earth is to preach Christ; to die is
to have an even closer union and experience of Christ.
It is tempting to die now, but it may mean more honor
to Christ if Paul lives. Christ is above life and death.
Whatever Christ wants. . .

## 28.  Jesus Alone Is Lord

Rom 14, 7-9
24A

None of us lives as his own master
and none of us dies as his own master.
While we live we are responsible to the Lord,
and when we die we die as his servants.
Both in life and in death we are the Lord's.
That is why Christ died and came to life again,
that he might be Lord
of both the dead and the living.

There was a problem, in Paul's day, about eating food
that had been sacrificed to idols in pagan temples. Some
felt they should not eat such meat, because of the religious connection; others, probably on the certainty that

33

the gods were "nothings," ate the food without a second thought. Paul here reprimands both groups for rashly judging each other.

His point is that none of us has any business judging anybody: *only Jesus is Lord*. We are not our own masters, either in life or death; we are totally in God's hands. His great gift of life should make all else relatively trivial.

It is to the Lord that we will have to render an account for what we do, not to each other.

## 29. Jesus Alone Is Our Riches

Phil 3, 8-14
5 Lent C

I have come to rate all as loss
in the light of the surpassing knowledge
of my Lord Jesus Christ.
For his sake I have forfeited everything;
I have accounted all else rubbish
so that Christ may be my wealth
and I may be in him,
not having any justice of my own
based on observance of the law.
The justice I possess
is that which comes through faith in Christ.
It has its origin in God and is based on faith.
I wish to know Christ
and the power flowing from his resurrection;
likewise to know how to share in his sufferings
by being formed into the pattern of his death.
Thus do I hope that I may arrive
at resurrection from the dead.
It is not that I have reached it yet,
or have already finished my course;
but I am racing to grasp the prize if possible,

since I have been grasped by Christ.
Brothers, I do not think of myself
as having reached the finish line.
I give no thought to what lies behind
but push on to what is ahead.
My entire attention is on the finish line
as I run toward the prize
to which God calls me—
life on high in Christ Jesus.

Paul, in the solitude of prison, contrasts his former values with the new life in Christ that he was given. The only worthwhile "gain" in his life is his present "knowledge" of Christ—intimate, deep relationship—and resurrection in him at the Second Coming. All else, by comparison, is "loss," rubbish. This new relationship came to him on the road to Damascus. As he constantly tells others, so Paul tells himself: salvation is entirely a gift of God, not something to be gained by works.

On our way to resurrection—none of us is perfectly "there" yet—we become more and more like Christ by living and suffering as he did. In Baptism we die to the world—"loss"—and are united to the living, suffering, rising Christ—"gain."

The power of Jesus is the source of our life. The final "prize" is to be found in Jesus when he comes. Meanwhile, holiness is the gift of being formed into his likeness.

## 30. Paul, a Prime Example of the Saving Mercy of Jesus

1 Tm 1, 12-17
24 C

I thank Christ Jesus our Lord,
who has strengthened me,

that he has made me his servant
and judged me faithful.
I was once a blasphemer, a persecutor,
a man filled with arrogance;
but because I did not know what I was doing in my
      unbelief,
I have been treated mercifully,
and the grace of our Lord
has been granted me in overflowing measure,
along with the faith and love
which are in Christ Jesus.
You can depend on this as worthy of full acceptance:
that Christ Jesus came into the world
to save sinners.
Of these I myself am the worst.
But on that very account
I was dealt with mercifully,
so that in me, as an extreme case,
Jesus Christ might display all his patience,
and that I might become an example
to those who would later have faith in him
and gain everlasting life.
To the King of ages,
the immortal, the invisible, the only God,
be honor and glory forever and ever!  Amen.

Paul himself is a prime example of the merciful salvation of God. He above all was included in the prayer of Jesus on the cross "to forgive them for they know not what they do." Paul "did not know what he was doing"—even though he was guilty of persecution. If *he* could be transformed by God's grace, all other sinners can surely hope for God's mercy. Indeed, the greatness of his sin was the measure of God's mercy.

Paul is reminding his hearers that it was not the Law that saved him. His conversion, his ministry, his faithfulness are all the gift of God, in Christ, destroying his self-righteousness, his misguided zeal, his reliance on mere human power.

# III. The Holy Spirit, the Gift

## 31. The Spirit Makes Us Children of God

Rom 8, 14 17
Trinity B

All who are led by the Spirit of God
are sons of God.
You did not receive a spirit of slavery
leading you back into fear,
but a spirit of adoption
through which
we cry out, "Abba!" (that is, "Father").
The Spirit himself gives witness with our spirit
that we are children of God.
But if we are children,
we are heirs as well:
heirs of God, heirs with Christ,
if only we suffer with him
so as to be glorified with him.

To be Christian is to call God *Father* (Abba) and Jesus *Lord*, and to do so entirely by the gift of the Spirit. It is the Spirit who makes us sons and daughters of the Father, and thus gives the word *father* a new meaning. By the active power of the Spirit, we share the sonship of Christ: we can speak to the Father as he did, as beloved children, his heirs.

For we are not slaves, but children of the Father. God is not our "owner." We are taken into the family of the Trinity. We cannot have the spirit of slaves when the personal Spirit (not merely our "spirit" or attitude) possesses us and enables us to cry out to the Father in trust, as Jesus did.

The Spirit witnesses to us, makes us conscious of our dignity. He empowers our prayer, which is itself a proof of God's love. The Spirit not only makes us children of the Father, but enables us to know this and to pray accordingly.

As beloved children we are heirs with Christ. He has already entered into possession of his "estate." We share his sonship, his rights—and his cross; therefore we shall also enter into glory with him.

## 32. The Spirit Is Our Assurance of God's Love for Us

Rom 5, 1-5
3 Lent A-a,
Trinity C

Now that we have been justified by faith,
we are at peace with God
through our Lord Jesus Christ.
Through him we have gained access by faith
to the grace in which we now stand,
and we boast of our hope
for the glory of God.
But not only that—
we even boast of our afflictions!
We know that affliction makes for endurance,
and endurance for tested virtue,
and tested virtue for hope.
And this hope will not leave us disappointed,
because the love of God
has been poured out in our hearts
through the Holy Spirit who has been given to us.

Paul reminds us that we are sure of eternal salvation.
Why? Because of the *experience* of peace and hope that
comes to us from the presence of the Holy Spirit within
us. God has made us holy—that is, "justified" us. This is
initial justification. Our final salvation is yet to come.
But because of this gift, we experience peace and hope.
God has graciously made us holy with his own holiness.
    We have the peace of being led by Christ into the
actual "royal chambers" of the Father. We live in his
presence. Yet there is still something to be hoped for,
and this hope is an absolutely certain one. Nothing can
shake it. It rests on the very love of God, who has

"flooded our inmost heart with love." (Paul is speaking here of God's love for us, not our love for God.) The subjective proof of this love from God is our experience of it, and realization of it, in the voice and witness of the Holy Spirit living within us. Thus God assures those whom he has made holy.

This assurance gives us perfect hope. It is based on God's love, which cannot deceive us. God has poured out his Spirit in us, and is present in us, lives in us. This has already happened. There is no end to the confidence this gives us!

### 33. The Spirit Lives in Us and Will Raise Us Up Forever

Rom 8, 8-11
14A,
5 Lent A-a

Those who are in the flesh
cannot please God.
But you are not in the flesh;
you are in the spirit,
since the Spirit of God dwells in you.
If anyone does not have the Spirit of Christ,
he does not belong to Christ.
If Christ is in you,
the body is indeed dead because of sin,
while the spirit lives because of justice.
If the Spirit of him who raised Jesus from the dead
    dwells in you,
then he who raised Christ from the dead
will bring your mortal bodies to life also
through his Spirit dwelling in you.

The Spirit of God was breathed into us at creation. Mankind lost that divine life by sin, and was limited to "flesh." For Paul "flesh" is the whole person of man

40

(not just the body) *on his own, self-centered*, trying to be *independent of God*, and thus separated from God and enslaved to sin. It is impossible for such a person to please God, no matter how "good" he thinks he is.

On the other hand, "spirit" for Paul means the whole person as possessed by the Spirit, God-oriented, alive with the life of God. If we are not thus "Spirit-ualized," we do not belong to Christ. Note that the Spirit of "God," of "Christ" and of "him who raised Jesus from the dead" are one and the same.

Those in whom the Spirit lives will be raised from the dead. In verse 10 there is a contrast between *body* (not "flesh" here), which will die because of mankind's sin, and *spirit* which is alive forever because of its union with the Spirit. As Jesus was raised to an entirely new existence by the Spirit of the Father, so the Christian will be raised to a new and eternal life.

## 34. A Spirit-Filled Life

Eph 5, 15-20
20B

Keep careful watch over your conduct.
Do not act like fools, but like thoughtful men.
Make the most of the present opportunity,
for these are evil days.
Do not continue in ignorance,
but try to discern the will of the Lord.
Avoid getting drunk on wine that leads to debauchery.
Be filled with the Spirit,
addressing one another in psalms and hymns and
    inspired songs.
Sing praise to the Lord with all your hearts.
Give thanks to God the Father
always and for everything

in the name of our Lord Jesus Christ.

Having exhorted the Church of Ephesus to let Christ shine on them, Paul continues to spell out the general attitude of a Christian: To be Christian is to be *filled with the Spirit*. Pagans become intoxicated with wine: Christians are to let the Spirit intoxicate them with the life of God.

This kind of "drunkenness" leads to thoughtful, prudent conduct. They are not to act like fools in the dark, not knowing what they are doing, but as men and women who have the light of Christ.

There is a sense of urgency: "Buy up the time!" The "time" of salvation (*kairos*) is here; the sinful world has nothing but evil days. Christians have light to discern the will of God in everyday situations.

Above all, Christian joy must be real and evident. Possessed by the Spirit who prays in them, Christians will show their joy in melodies that delight men and honor God, especially songs of praise and appreciation of the Father's goodness.

### 35. Christian Life in the Spirit—or Death in Sin

Rom 8, 12-13
14A

We are debtors, then, my brothers—
but not to the flesh,
so that we should live according to the flesh.
If you live according to the flesh,
you will die;
but if by the spirit
you put to death the evil deeds of the body,
you will live.

We are no longer slaves to being "flesh"—that is, persons cut off from God by their own attempt to be independent of God, self-centered, "masters of their own fate." In this condition we are inclined to sin and then be trapped in it. In such persons, eternal death has already happened to their spirit—and will someday happen to their whole person.

But if we open ourselves, the Spirit puts to death evil deeds and their effects, all our "fleshly" independence. Now our whole person, body-spirit, is alive and does "Spirit-ual" deeds.

It is still possible for the Christian to be tempted to be "flesh." Only the power of the Spirit freely accepted can control these temptations.

## 36. All Gifts of the Spirit Are for Our Unity

1 Cor 12, 3-7.12-13
2C-a
Pentecost

No one can say: "Jesus is Lord,"
except in the Holy Spirit,
There are different gifts but the same Spirit;
there are different ministries but the same Lord;
there are different works but the same God
who accomplishes all of them in every one.
To each person
the manifestation of the Spirit
is given for the common good.
The body is one and has many members,
but all the members,
many though they are, are one body;
and so it is with Christ.
It was in one Spirit that all of us,
whether Jew or Greek, slave or free,
were baptized into one body.

**All of us have been given to drink
of the one Spirit.**

Paul is speaking of how to judge the various special
gifts that have been received by individuals in the Corinthian Church. He is leading up to insisting that a life of
love is the primary gift of all.

First, it is certainly a gift of the Spirit to be able to
acknowledge the fundamental belief of Christianity,
that Jesus is Lord. Truly to believe in Jesus is a sign of
the Spirit's presence.

Other *gifts* we receive differ from person to person,
but our goodwill and sincerity unite us, even though we
act as differently as eyes and hands. There are also differing *ministries*, or services, in the Church, but they are all
from one Servant, Jesus. There are differing *works* from
the one Father who empowers all. But the greatest gift
is *the* Gift, the Spirit.

If anyone values his or her individual gifts in a super-
cilious way, he is contradicting the Spirit and the unity
of love which the Spirit forms. The Spirit never leads to
the uncharity and factions present in the Church of
Corinth.

The purpose of the gifts is the common good of the
whole Body of Christ. Gifts are means to loving others.

Above all other considerations, therefore, is the need
for the unity of charity. Just as each member of our
body should be beneficial for the working of the whole
body, so it is with the Body of Christ.

The Spirit joining us together in love makes other
considerations relatively unimportant; for instance,
whether we are slaves or free, Jews or Greeks, etc. We
have all drunk baptismally from the one Spirit, becoming members of the one Body.

# 37. Particular Gifts of the Spirit

1 Cor 12, 8-11
2 C-b

To one the Spirit gives wisdom in discourse,
to another the power to express knowledge.
Through the Spirit one receives faith;
by the same Spirit another is given the gift of healing,
and still another miraculous powers.
Prophecy is given to one;
to another power to distinguish one spirit from another.
One receives the gift of tongues,
another that of interpreting the tongues.
But it is one and the same Spirit
who produces all these gifts,
distributing them to each as he wills.

Paul's list of special gifts puts the favorite of the Corinthians last—the gift of tongues. Again, Paul is leading up to his emphasis on the fact that charity is the greatest gift of all.

1) *Wisdom*, probably the gift of discovering and explaining the deepest Christian truth. It is not what great theologians acquire "naturally," though of course they may have the gift. 2) *Knowledge*, the gift of teaching and applying the faith practically for others. 3) *Faith*, here the special gift that moves mountains. 4) *Healing* of persons physically, spiritually. 5) *The power to work miracles.* 6) *Prophecy*, the gift of speaking for God, proclaiming his word, awakening the consciences of people. 7) *Discernment of spirits*, the ability to judge correctly whether gifts are from God or from another source. 8) *Tongues*, the gift of glorifying God in ecstatic sounds that are not intelligible. 9) *Interpretation of tongues*, the gift of explaining the rapturous expressions of those who pray in tongues.

## 38. The Purpose of the Church: to Be an Open Letter to the World

2 Cor 3, 1-3
8B-a

Am I beginning to speak well of myself again?
Do I need letters of recommendation
to you or from you
as others might?
You are my letter,
known and read by all men,
written on your hearts.
Clearly you are a letter of Christ
which I have delivered,
a letter written not with ink
but by the Spirit of the living God,
not on tablets of stone
but on tablets of flesh in the heart.

What is the Church? It is the Body of Christ, the temple of the Holy Spirit, the Bride. It is Christ visibly working in the world today. It is a letter to the world, written by God through his apostles. The Church has a simple purpose: to show the world how much God loves all people. It is the glory and the scandal of the Church that it both succeeds and fails in its mission.

Paul apparently had been accused of being too much his own letter of recommendation. He replies to the charge by saying that he doesn't even need such a letter. The Church in Corinth, for all its problems, is enough. The healing and love that God has brought there, making a strong Christian community in a corrupt city, is an open letter for all to read.

It is not Paul, of course, who writes the letter, but Christ. He is merely the scribe. The Spirit writes the letter of faith on their hearts.

Christians do not prove by argument that Christ is the Savior of the world: they show his saving grace in their lives.

## 39. The Church: a Community Called Together

1 Cor 1, 1-3
2A

Paul, called by God's will to be an apostle of Christ
    Jesus,
and Sosthenes our brother,
send greetings to the Church of God
which is in Corinth;
to you who have been consecrated
in Christ Jesus
and called to be a holy people,
as to all those who, wherever they may be,
call on the name of our Lord Jesus Christ,
their Lord and ours.
Grace and peace from God our Father
and the Lord Jesus Christ.

The Church of Corinth is an *ekklesia*—a community
called together by God.

They have been made holy, consecrated, sanctified,
by being incorporated into the Body of Christ in faith.
They are (by God's gift and not their own merits) "a
holy people gathered together," a chosen people. They
are the new Israel, a sacred assembly, the community of
the Lord.

Paul delicately combines an old Hebrew greeting,
"Shalom!" (peace), and "Grace!" (charis), a word familiar
to the Gentiles.

But the holy Church is not perfectly holy. There are
rugged individualists and unpleasant situations which
Paul will have to deal with at Corinth. Therefore he also
asserts his authority as an authentic apostle, divinely
called.

### 40. Every Human Being
### Is Called to Christ's Body, the Church

Eph 3, 2-3.5-6
Epiphany

I am sure you have heard of the ministry
which God in his goodness gave me in your regard.
God's secret plan, as I have briefly described it,
was revealed to me,
unknown to men in former ages
but now revealed by the Spirit
to the holy apostles and prophets.
It is no less than this: in Christ Jesus
the Gentiles are now co-heirs with the Jews,
members of the same body
and sharers of the promise
through the preaching of the gospel.

The Gospel story of the Magi coming to Bethlehem is symbolic of the inclusion of Gentiles in God's eternal plan to give himself to his creatures. It was unthinkable to the Jews of Jesus' time that Gentiles—pagans, outsiders—could be admitted on an equal basis with Jews in an entirely new Israel, in a new covenant. Yet, Paul says, this was God's plan from eternity, now revealed by the Holy Spirit through official witnesses like himself. The entire world is to be the Church. Everyone is called to be the Chosen People, the Body of Christ.

Paul even makes up words to convey the amazingness of the new unity. Jew and Gentile (man and woman, black and white, East and West) are called to be *co-heirs*, *co-members* of the same Body, *co-sharers* in the same promises.

## 41. A Model Church

1 Thes 1, 5-10
30A

You know as well as we do
what we proved to be like
when, while still among you,
we acted on your behalf.
You, in turn, became imitators of us
and of the Lord
receiving the word despite great trials,
with the joy that comes from the Holy Spirit.
Thus you became a model
for all the believers of Macedonia and Achaia.
The word of the Lord
has echoed forth from you resoundingly.
This is true not only in Macedonia and Achaia;
throughout every region your faith in God is celebrated,
which makes it needless for us to say anything more.
The people of those parts are reporting
what kind of reception we had from you
and how you turned to God from idols
to serve him who is the living and true God
and to await from heaven
the Son he raised from the dead—Jesus,
who delivers us from the wrath to come.

The converts in Thessalonia are models for other
Christian Churches. Paul praises their faith and courage,
and tells of their faith wherever he goes.

With no false humility, Paul says that the unselfish
and fearless way he and his companions preached to and
lived among them was a sure indication of the active and
powerful presence of the Holy Spirit.

The Spirit has created a Church through the apostolic
preaching (kerygma) of which we have here a brief sum-
mary. They became a Church by a) accepting the one
living God by turning from idols (evidently most Thessalonians were pagans); b) believing in Jesus as Son of God,
risen Savior; c) preparing for and looking forward to the

Second Coming when Jesus rescues us from the final manifestation of the wrath of God against sin; d) embracing the faith even in the face of persecution.

In their suffering, the Thessalonians experienced a joy that could be traced only to the Holy Spirit. This suffering is the way to salvation, in imitation of Jesus himself.

Thus, to be "Church" is to turn to the one God, in Jesus, and to prepare for his coming by sharing in his suffering.

### 42. The Sevenfold Oneness of the Church

Eph 4, 1-6
17B

I plead with you as a prisoner for the Lord,
to live a life worthy of the calling you have received,
with perfect humility, meekness, and patience,
bearing with one another lovingly.
Make every effort to preserve the unity
which has the Spirit as its origin
and peace as its binding force.
There is but one body and one Spirit,
just as there is but one hope
given all of you by your call.
There is one Lord, one faith, one baptism,
one God and Father of all, who is over all,
and works through all, and is in all.

The Spirit is the source of all loving unity between person and person, between humanity and God.

The sevenfold formula of Church unity is: one *Body*—the visible community, the sign of Christ; one *Spirit*—the inner source of the one life; one *hope*—because of the promise of the Spirit; one *Lord*—Jesus, the glorified, victorious Kyrios; one *faith*—personal

adherence to Christ and also to the body of doctrine
which records the content of faith; one *Baptism* into the
one Christ—one death to sin, one life to God; one *God
and Father* of one family, seated at the one Table.

The Church already has this basic unity, and it cannot
be lost. Yet it is a unity that must always be achieved
and perfected. Christians must live out their oneness in
God.

### 43. The Body of Christ: Unity and Variety

1 Cor 12, 12-26
3 C-a

The body is one and has many members,
but all the members, many though they are,
are one body; and so it is with Christ.
It was in one Spirit that all of us,
whether Jew or Greek, slave or free,
were baptized into one body.
All of us have been given to drink
of the one Spirit.
Now the body is not one member, it is many.
If the foot should say,
"Because I am not a hand I do not belong to the body,"
would it then no longer belong to the body?
If the ear should say,
"Because I am not an eye I do not belong to the body,"
would it then no longer belong to the body?
If the body were all eye,
what would happen to our hearing?
If it were all ear
what would happen to our smelling?
As it is, God has set each member of the body
in the place he wanted it to be.
If all the members were alike,
where would the body be?

There are, indeed, many different members,
but one body.
The eye cannot say to the hand,
"I do not need you,"
any more than the head can say to the feet,
"I do not need you."
Even those members of the body which seem less
    important
are in fact indispensable.
We honor the members we consider less honorable
by clothing them with greater care,
thus bestowing on the less presentable
a propriety which the more presentable already have.
God has so constructed the body
as to give greater honor to the lowly members,
that there may be no dissension in the body,
but that all the members
may be concerned for one another.
If one member suffers,
all the members suffer with it;
if one member is honored,
all the members share its joy.

Christ makes us, the Church, *one* Body—his Mystical Body. Unity is paramount; yet variety is as necessary as it is in the functioning of our one physical body. Each member of the Church contributes to the healthy functioning of the whole.

The unity of the Mystical Body is not merely an organizational or external unity, but also an inner unity of love. Christ alone creates the unity of love in his Body.

In one sense the unity is all-important. When the Spirit baptizes us into the life of God, that fact outshines any accidental differences—whether we are black or white, male or female, Russian or Chinese.

Yet the unity is not dull and monolithic. There is infinite variety in the Church, by the gifts of the Spirit. The variety is not merely a pleasant one, but a functional one.

Not all of us have official positions in the Church, but each of us is like a member of the human body. The tip of our little finger seems unimportant—until it is injured. But again, unity: if any member tries to be the whole body, or to function independently of the body, the whole body suffers.

Paul is putting the charismatic gifts in perspective. He reminds the "gifted" ones of Corinth that, just as we give greater honor to the more lowly members of our body, so perhaps the fact that some have an abundance of charismatic gifts may indicate that they are the "weaker" members of the Body of Christ!

Variety and specialness should contribute to unity, not to pride.

## 44. Organizational and Charismatic Gifts

1 Cor 12, 27-30
3 C-b

You, then, are the body of Christ.
Every one of you is a member of it.
Furthermore, God has set up in the church
first apostles, second prophets, third teachers,
then miracle workers, healers, assistants,
administrators, and those who speak in tongues.
Are all apostles? Are all prophets?
Are all teachers?
Do all work miracles
or have the gift of healing?
Do all speak in tongues,
all have the gift of interpretation of tongues?

Christians form the Church, the Body of Christ, just as our various organs form our human body, and each has his or her own role to play.

God has established in his Church a hierarchy of functions. Paul now lists these gifts in the order of their importance. First, the gift of being an *apostle*, on whom and through whom Christ founds and guides the Church; second, the gift of being a *prophet*, inspired to preach the word of God; third, the gift of being a *catechist*, providing regular instruction in the Church.

After these come the lesser gifts: the gift of working *miracles*, signs which lead to faith or confirm believers in the faith; the gift of *healing* infirmities; the gift of *helping*, through works of charity; the gift of *administering* the Churches; the gift of *tongues*.

Though the organization of the Church was still developing, there was already at Corinth some skeletal ruling organization. Some of the gifts are "institutional," that is, they belong to the official organizational structure of the Church: guides, teachers. Other gifts are "charismatic," that is, given for the good of the whole Church to individuals who may or may not have an official position in the Church. For Paul, of course, there can be no conflict here, because all gifts are given for the Church's unity in charity.

### 45. Unity in Christ as Sons and Daughters of the Father

Gal 3, 26-29
12C

Each one of you is a son of God
because of your faith in Christ Jesus.
All of you who have been baptized into Christ
have clothed yourselves with him.
There does not exist among you
Jew or Greek, slave or freeman,
male or female.

All are one in Christ Jesus.
Furthermore, if you belong to Christ
you are the descendants of Abraham,
which means you inherit
all that was promised.

Paul is arguing for the new era of faith and freedom,
as against the condition of being under the Law. Both
Jewish and Gentile Christians are now sons and daughters
of God, no longer under slavery to sin and death. This
birth into being children of God takes place at Baptism,
a public manifestation of God's creative love.

Filled with baptismal faith, we are clothed with
Christ; we take on his life, and gradually his disposition
and attitude. As his brothers and sisters, we have a unity
in love which makes all other labels secondary or irrele-
vant: whether we are male or female, this nationality or
that, this social condition or that.

In addition, as brothers and sisters of Christ, we are
the heirs Abraham was promised. Christ fulfills the
promise made to Abraham: there is no further need of
Law, for it has been fulfilled and transformed.

### 46. Unity Based on the Humble Attitude of Christ

Phil 2, 1-5
26A-a

In the name of the encouragement
you owe me in Christ,
in the name of the solace that love can give,
of fellowship in spirit, compassion, and pity,
I beg you:  make my joy complete
by your unanimity, possessing the one love,
united in spirit and ideals.
Never act out of rivalry or conceit;
rather, let all parties think humbly of others

as superior to themselves,
each of you looking to others' interests
rather than his own.

Before Paul's great statement on the emptying and
exaltation of Christ, he pleads with the Church at
Philippi to have a unity based on selfless humility, like
that of Christ.

He identifies four attitudes that should be found in
the daily life of Christians: 1) *encouragement* (*para-
clesis*, from which our word *paraclete* comes), a "side-
by-side-ness" of mutual support; 2) *solace*, the cheering
verbal exchanges that loving people make; 3) *fellowship*
(*koinonia*, community), a oneness of persons who
share ideals and spirit; 4) *compassion*, a gut-level attention to others' needs.

Paul hopes to have the joy of seeing their double
unity of heart and mind, an absence of rivalry and self-
centeredness. In short, a Christians's attitude should be
as loving-humble as that of Christ.

### 47.  Remedy for Dissension:
### Awareness of God's Gifts and Call.

1 Cor 1, 3-9
1 Advent B

Grace and peace from God our Father
and the Lord Jesus Christ.
I continually thank my God for you
because of the favor he has bestowed on you
in Christ Jesus,
in whom you have been richly endowed
with every gift of speech and knowledge.
Likewise, the witness I bore to Christ
has been so confirmed among you

that you lack no spiritual gift
as you wait for the revelation of our Lord Jesus.
He will strengthen you to the end,
so that you will be blameless
on the day of our Lord Jesus Christ.
God is faithful,
and it was he who called you to fellowship
with his Son, Jesus Christ our Lord.

These verses precede Paul's fraternal correction of
the tense and faction-ridden Church at Corinth. He lays
the groundwork for a solution of the problem: a realization of their high calling, and the generosity of a faithful God. Paul is making a positive statement of the true
nature of Christian life.

Abundant grace has been given them, and Paul thanks
God for the high gifts they have received: charismatic
gifts of speech and knowledge—in fact, *every* "spiritual
gift." Their life is a waiting in faith and love for the
coming of Jesus. As they wait, God will strengthen them
for all he calls them to do, because he is a faithful God.
His love never changes, no matter how ours does. He
will make it possible for them to be blameless when
Jesus comes.

### 48. The Church Must Not Split Into Factions

1 Cor 1, 10-13.17
3A

I beg you, brothers,
in the name of our Lord Jesus Christ,
to agree in what you say.
Let there be no factions;
rather, be united in mind and judgment.
I have been informed, my brothers,
by certain members of Chloe's household

that you are quarreling among yourselves.
This is what I mean:  One of you will say,
"I belong to Paul,"
another, "I belong to Apollos,"
still another, "Cephas has my allegiance,"
and  the fourth, "I belong to Christ."
Has Christ, then, been divided into parts?
Was it Paul who was crucified for you?
Was it in Paul's name that you were baptized?
Christ did not send me to baptize
but to preach the gospel—
not with wordy "wisdom," however,
lest the cross of Christ
be rendered void of its meaning!

Paul pleads for unity in Christ, against the cliques or factions that had come into existence.

The factions were not a matter of dogmatic difference, but of personal loyalties. Apollos, a well-educated Alexandrian Jew, probably appealed to the educated minority. Peter perhaps drew partisan followers from Palestinian Jews from the "mother Church" at Jerusalem. Paul no doubt was claimed by the majority of his converts at Corinth. A "Christ party" (if there was one) claimed special relationship to Christ, possibly from actually knowing him. Paul (1 Cor 16, 12) does not blame Apollos or Peter.

Paul pleads for "perfect agreement"—a compromising on non-essentials  and a unity of outlook and purpose. It does not matter *who* baptizes:  Christ is the only source.

Paul is not deprecating Baptism:  like Jesus, he probably had his helpers do the baptizing. Conversions certainly did not come from his poor and simple preaching, but only through the power of the cross of Christ.

## 49. Disunity Does Violence to God Himself

1 Cor 3, 16-23
7A

Are you not aware
that you are the temple of God,
and that the Spirit of God dwells in you?
If anyone destroys God's temple,
God will destroy him.
For the temple of God is holy,
and you are that temple.
Let no one delude himself.
If any one of you thinks he is wise in a worldly way,
he had better become a fool.
In that way he will really be wise,
for the wisdom of this world
is absurdity with God.
Scripture says, "He catches the wise in their craftiness";
and again, "The Lord knows how empty are the
        thoughts of the wise."
Let there be no boasting about men.
All things are yours, whether it be Paul,
or Apollos, or Cephas, or the world,
or life, or death, or the present, or the future:
all these are yours,
and you are Christ's
and Christ is God's.

Paul is reproaching the Corinthians for the factions
that have spoiled the unity of the Church of Corinth.
The community there is the dwelling place of God.
(Later, in 6, 19, the individual is also said to be the
dwelling place of God.) Promoters of factions are banish-
ing the Spirit and destroying the building. This is sacri-
legious, for Christians are consecrated to God. It does
violence to God himself, and will destroy those who are
guilty of it.

The Corinthians are immature as Christians—even
fools. They are judging by merely worldly standards.
Overconfident in their judgment, they are trusting in

men rather than God. The famous preachers—Paul, Peter, Apollos—are *for the people*; the people are not *for them*. Everything is for the people of God—the world, life, death, the present and the future. Everything belongs to them—but they belong to Christ, not to human leaders. It is by union with Christ, not by divisions, that they will share these goods.

### 50. Authorities in the Church Are Christ's Servants

1 Cor 4, 1-5
8A

Men should regard us as servants of Christ
and administrators of the mysteries of God.
The first requirement of an administrator
is that he prove trustworthy.
It matters little to me
whether you or any human court pass judgment on me.
I do not even pass judgment on myself.
Mind you, I have nothing on my conscience.
But that does not mean that I am declaring myself
    innocent.
The Lord is the one to judge me,
so stop passing judgment before the time of his return.
He will bring to light what is hidden in darkness
and manifest the intentions of hearts.
At that time, everyone will receive his praise from God.

It is a great misunderstanding to make preachers into cult figures, as the factions in Corinth did. The apostles are merely Christ's assistants and managers. They oversee and distribute the treasures of truth and the saving gospel life. They are administering someone else's property—God's—and he demands they be trustworthy and wholly devoted to divine interests.

Paul is acting only for Christ, and will answer to him.

His conscience is clear, yet he humbly admits the possibility of self-deception. "No one is a judge in his own case" applies to him too, and he is willing to leave the judgment up to Christ. But, in the meantime, he will be indifferent to human approval or disapproval.

At his coming, Christ will reveal the motives people had in their acts and attitudes and will assess their merits. Since he is the only infallible judge, judgment should be left to him.

## 51. Authority in the Church: Courageous Service

2 Tim 3, 14—4, 2
29C

You must remain faithful
to what you have learned and believed,
because you know who your teachers were.
Likewise, from your infancy you have known the sacred
      Scriptures,
the source of the wisdom
which through faith in Jesus Christ leads to salvation.
All Scripture is inspired of God
and is useful for teaching—
for reproof, correction, and training in holiness
so that the man of God may be fully competent
and equipped for every good work.
In the presence of God and of Christ Jesus,
who is coming to judge the living and the dead,
and by his appearing and his kingly power,
I charge you to preach the word,
to stay with this task
whether convenient or inconvenient—
correcting, reproving, appealing—
constantly teaching and never losing patience.

Paul is reminding Timothy to exercise the ministry of the word to the fullest degree, even at the cost of great

inconvenience. He must have the courage to lead, like
Paul, in spite of opposition.

His leadership and authority requires, first of all,
faithfulness to what he has been taught. His teachers
were his mother and grandmother, Lois and Eunice
(2 Tim 1, 5; 2, 2; 3, 10). Another source of strength
and faithfulness is Scripture. (Paul is referring to the Old
Testament here. It would be difficult to say how much
of the New Testament had been written, or, if written,
recognized as inspired at the time of this letter.) Paul is
very definite in his conviction of the divine origin of the
Scriptures and of their value.

This key passage indicates general ways Church
authority can use Scripture—instruction, pointing out
errors, correcting, educating in holiness and truth.

A final motive for Timothy's courageous ministry is
that he will, like all authorities, appear before Christ,
the Judge of the living and the dead.

### 52. Paul's Authority

Gal 1, 1-2.6-10
9C

Paul, an apostle sent not by men or by any man,
but by Jesus Christ and God his Father
who raised him from the dead—
I and my brothers who are with me,
send greetings to the Churches in Galatia.
I am amazed that you are so soon deserting him who
    called you
in accord with his gracious design in Christ,
and are going over to another gospel.
But there is no other.
Some who wish to alter the gospel of Christ
must have confused you.
For if even we or an angel from heaven

should preach to you a gospel
not in accord with the one we delivered to you,
let a curse be upon him!
I repeat what I have just said:
if anyone preaches a gospel to you
other than the one you received,
let a curse be upon him!
Whom would you say I am trying to please at this
      point—men or God?
Is this how I seek to ingratiate myself with men?
If I were trying to win man's approval,
I would surely not be serving Christ!

Paul again claims apostolic authority. He is directly appointed, equal to the Twelve, a representative sent with full powers to perform a definite task. His authority is from God, unlike that claimed by false teachers whose authority is from men. Notice that his primary witness is of the resurrection.

He is shocked that his converts in Galatia have so soon or so easily adopted the spurious "gospel" of those who held that the Mosaic Law and circumcision were as necessary as faith in Christ. The true gospel is a power emanating from Christ. It is one as Christ is one. Even an angel teaching otherwise is to be spurned. (Paul is referring to a Jewish opinion that the Law was given to men by angels.)

Such teachers should be regarded as "anathema"— cursed, excommunicated, excluded from the Kingdom. Paul uses his authority to thus exclude and "curse" them.

He also feels compelled to defend his use of authority against the charge that he is guilty of compromise and inconsistency. His sternness, he seems to say, is hardly that of a man trying to win friends at any cost.

## 53. The Church and the Jews

Rom 9, 1-5
19A

I speak the truth in Christ: I do not lie.
My conscience bears me witness in the Holy Spirit
that there is great grief and constant pain in my heart.
Indeed, I could even wish
to be separated from Christ
for the sake of my brothers,
my kinsmen the Israelites.
Theirs were the adoption, the glory,
the covenants, the lawgiving,
the worship, and the promises;
theirs were the patriarchs,
and from them came the Messiah
(I speak of his human origins).
Blessed forever be God who is over all! Amen.

Paul grieves for his fellow Israelites who were favored
with the great external signs of God's loving presence,
but who were not ready to receive Christ in faith.

He could wish to be separated (anathema) from Christ
if this would save his Jewish brothers and sisters. Moses
had used nearly the same language (Ex 32) after the
worship of the golden calf. Both cases show a vehement
sense of intercession for blood brothers.

Israel's privileges should have led them to Christ: a)
their *adoption* as children of God (Ex 4, 22; Hos 11, 1);
b) the manifested *glory* of God at Sinai and in the temple—the sign of his very presence; c) the *covenants* God
made with Abraham, Jacob, Moses; d) God's giving of
the *Law*, the manifestation of his loving will; e) the *worship* he himself prescribed for them; f) God's *promises*
of the Messiah to them; g) the honor of having the
*patriarchs*—a history, a tradition, a plan; h) the *Messiah*
himself. (Paul's conviction and prayer about the future
of Israel is found in Rom 11, 23-32.)

## 54. The Jews Are God's Beloved People

Rom 11, 13-15. 29-32
20A

I say this now to you Gentiles:
Inasmuch as I am the apostle of the Gentiles,
I glory in my ministry,
trying to rouse my fellow Jews to envy and save some
    of them.
For if their rejection has meant reconciliation for the
    world,
what will their acceptance mean?
Nothing less than life from the dead!
God's gifts and his call are irrevocable.
Just as you were once disobedient to God
and now have received mercy through their disobedience,
so they have become disobedient—
since God wished to show you mercy—
that they too may receive mercy.
God has imprisoned all in disobedience
that he might have mercy on all.

Paul has been reminding his Gentile converts that
Israel's rejection of Christ is evidence of God's grace,
and not a reason for hatred or pride. Paul is still a Jew,
passionately desirous of bringing his Jewish brothers and
sisters to Christ. Their rejection of Christ was the occasion of the Gentiles' receiving him. When the Jews turn
to him, there will be new life for them.

It is important to note Paul's insistence that God's
gifts and his call (to the Jews) is irrevocable. It stands.
They are his beloved people. He continues to exercise
his steadfast covenant love and mercy toward them. In
the Old Testament, the Gentiles seemed to be "outside."
Now the Jews seem to be "outside." Human disobedience is, in any case, only the basis for even more merciful intervention on the part of God. Sin provides God
with the occasion of showing his infinite mercy,
whether to individuals or groups.

## 55. The Chosen People: a Warning to the Church

1 Cor 10, 1-6. 10-12
3 Lent C

I want you to remember this:
our fathers were all under the cloud
and all passed through the sea;
by the cloud and the sea
all of them were baptized into Moses.
All ate the same spiritual food.
All drank the same spiritual drink
(they drank from the spiritual rock that was following
    them,
and the rock was Christ),
yet we know that God was not pleased with most of
    them,
for "they were struck down in the desert."
These things happened as an example
to keep us from wicked desires such as theirs.
Nor are you to grumble as some of them did,
to be killed by the destroying angel.
The things that happened to them
serve as an example.
They have been written as a warning to us,
upon whom the end of the ages has come.
For all these reasons,
let anyone who thinks he is standing upright
watch out lest he fall!

Though the Church, the Body of Christ, cannot perish,
it can be damaged by the sin of its members, and individuals can lose their inheritance entirely. Paul uses the
punishment of the Chosen People as a warning to Christians.

First, the Chosen People had a kind of Baptism: the
water through which they escaped to freedom and the
cloud that guided and covered them in the desert—a
symbol of God's saving presence. Their baptismal immersion "into" Moses delivered them from slavery and
formed them into God's people instead of a collection

of tribes. Christians are baptized into Christ and thereby made into his people, one Mystical Body.

Second, the Chosen People had a kind of Eucharist: water from the rock and the daily gift of manna. The Sinai covenant had a meal that prefigured the Meal of the New Covenant. Paul uses a legend of the rabbis about a rock that actually followed the Israelites in the desert. In truth, Christ, though not yet born, was the source of their being saved from slavery.

Yet most of the Chosen People, despite these privileges, died without entering the Promised Land—because of their sin, because God says, "They have put me to the test ten times and have failed to heed my voice." Christians are thereby warned against trusting in an automatic salvation through Baptism and Eucharist, and against thinking they are "standing upright" by their own power.

# IV. The Christian Life-
# Our Dying and Rising With Christ

## A. THE CROSS AND SUFFERING

### 56. Suffering: Living Out
Our Baptismal Death and Resurrection

2 Tm 2, 8-13
28C

Remember that Jesus Christ,
a descendant of David,
was raised from the dead.
This is the gospel I preach;
in preaching it I suffer as a criminal,
even to the point of being thrown into chains—
but there is no chaining the word of God!
Therefore I bear with all of this
for the sake of those whom God has chosen,
in order that they may obtain the salvation
to be found in Christ Jesus
and with it eternal glory.
You can depend on this:
If we have died with him
we shall also live with him;
If we hold out to the end
we shall also reign with him.
But if we deny him he will deny us.
If we are unfaithful he will still remain faithful;
for he cannot deny himself.

The author summarizes the gospel: the death and
resurrection of Jesus leads to eternal glory. The path
leads through the suffering of Christ shared by his
members.

It is an impassioned pointing to the end: Look at the

absolutely certain hope you have! You will have salvation. You will be admitted to the inaccessible glory of God, made visible in Jesus. You now share and you will share in the very life of God himself!

Verses 11-12 seem to be from a baptismal hymn. The reference, though, is not merely to the dying and rising of Baptism, but also to the development of this experience in the Christian life, especially in the trials and sufferings of the apostolate. Paul suffers for proclaiming the Good News, and his suffering is joined to that of Christ for the good of all his brothers and sisters.

So also the Christian must maintain the courage of hope, for if we are unwilling to pay the price of belonging to Christ, he will have no choice but to "deny" us; that is, he cannot recognize us as his followers. But the whole power of Christ is engaged in preventing that ultimate tragedy. He is faithful even when we are unfaithful. There is nothing else he can do; for it is his nature to be merciful; he cannot be untrue to his nature.

## 57. The Crucified Christ Is Our Power and Wisdom

1 Cor 1, 22-25
3 Lent B

Jews demand "signs"
and Greeks look for "wisdom,"
but we preach Christ crucified,
a stumbling block to Jews,
and an absurdity to Gentiles;
but to those who are called,
Jews and Greeks alike,
Christ is the power of God
and the wisdom of God.
For God's folly is wiser than men,
and his weakness more powerful than men.

In reprimanding the Corinthian Church for its factions, Paul comes to consider what real wisdom is: all men, Jews and Gentiles alike, had a false view of it; it is a paradoxical reality.

The Jews unwisely expected God to make an evident and dazzling intervention ("signs") to bring their nation to its rightful ascendancy and power. But Jesus gave "signs" that could be read only by pure faith. So the Jews were scandalized by the gospel message of a crucified Messiah as God's "sign." The idea of the Messiah undergoing the degradation of crucifixion was disgusting to the Jewish mind.

The Gentiles (Greeks) unwisely expected a perfectly rational and humanly satisfying explanation of all things ("wisdom"), precluding the need for faith. So they saw the gospel as foolishness. What kind of God could "reasonably" go through that? How could they "reasonably" accept such a one's claim?

Those whom God gives the gift of a call to faith—that is, who hear and respond—receive real wisdom: They can see and commit themselves to the crucified and risen Christ. They see the great sign and have the real wisdom. God's foolishness and futile gesture turn out to be perfectly wise, "reasonable" and the most powerful and dazzling sign ever given.

Death is not some external punishment God applied to sin (as if he could have done something else). It is the inevitable result of sin. But death (in Christ and those who die with him) is now the most perfect and inevitable sign of total love and obedience to God.

## 58. The Cross, Our Only Hope

Gal 6, 14-18
14C

May I never boast of anything
but the cross of our Lord Jesus Christ!
Through it, the world has been crucified to me
and I to the world.
It means nothing whether one is circumcised or not.
All that matters is that one is created anew.
Peace and mercy on all
who follow this rule of life,
and on the Israel of God.
Henceforth, let no man trouble me,
for I bear the brand marks of Jesus in my body.
Brothers, may the favor of our Lord Jesus Christ
be with your spirit. Amen.

Paul concludes his scathing denunciation of the "Juda-izers," those who tried to impose circumcision and other legal requirements of the Old Testament on Gentile converts. He is attacking those who soft-pedaled the message of the Cross and advocated circumcision to avoid censure and persecution. He insists that circumcision—or the lack of it—means nothing. The only thing we rely on ("boast of") is the cross of Christ.

The cross is singled out because, first, it is the perfect manifestation of Christ's self-giving. Second, the dedication to God which it signifies is opposed to the "world"—that is, all who are hostile to God. Finally, its marks on the body of Christ are the answer to the mark of circumcision. The world's power is broken on Calvary, and we are set free internally. The world is crucified; the enemies of God are "dead" as far as real power is concerned; and we are crucified to the world by a total turn-around in values.

Positively, the Christian is crucified by being united to the saving work of Christ by Baptism and faith and is created anew—that is, transformed in the very core of his being—by the risen Christ and through his Spirit. This is the Christian "rule of life."

Paul's own life shows how the transforming crucifixion becomes visible. His illnesses, stoning, floggings for the sake of the gospel are the "brand marks of Jesus."

### 59.  Christian Holiness Involves Suffering as Christ Did

Col 1, 24-28
16C

Even now I find my joy
in the suffering I endure for you.
In my own flesh I fill up
what is lacking in the sufferings of Christ
for the sake of his body, the church.
I became a minister of this Church
through the commission God gave me
to preach among you his word in its fullness,
that mystery hidden from ages and generations past
but now revealed to his holy ones.
God has willed to make known to them
the glory beyond price
which this mystery brings to the Gentiles—
the mystery of Christ in you, your hope of glory.
This is the Christ we proclaim
while we admonish all men and teach them
in the full measure of wisdom,
hoping to make every man complete in Christ.

Since we are one with Christ, we form a Church in which we suffer for one another.

Paul is establishing his relationship with the entire community. This relationship is one of being happy even in the messianic sufferings—that is, in sharing in the birth pangs of a new era as the plan of God comes to birth.

Christ comes to the "holy ones" who accept the message in faith and are incorporated into his Body by Baptism; thus we receive a pledge and absolute hope of eternal glory. This is for everyone (Paul says it three times), in contrast to the pagan mysteries which are only for the select few.

Paul has the task and also the great power of proclaiming this mystery-now-revealed, so that men may have full maturity in Christ. Thus he can "fill up what is lacking in the sufferings of Christ." One explanation: The Church—people—is always far from realizing its full maturity. There is always a "holiness gap" between what it is and what it can and will be. In filling this gap, Christians must constantly grow. But their very growing in virtue—which must include proclaiming Christ in apostolic witness—will bring opposition. Jesus said that his coming would bring the sword, not peace.

His suffering is the first and final difference between sin and salvation. But we need to share with him, to become one with his rejection, his endurance, his cross.

### 60. Suffering Shows the Power of Christ in Us

2 Cor 4, 6-11
9B

God, who said, "Let light shine out of darkness,"
has shone in our hearts,
that we in turn might make known
the glory of God shining on the face of Christ.
This treasure we possess in earthen vessels
to make it clear that its surpassing power
comes from God and not from us.
We are afflicted in every way possible,
but we are not crushed;
full of doubts, we never despair.

We are persecuted but never abandoned;
we are struck down but never destroyed.
Continually we carry about in our bodies
the dying of Jesus
so that in our bodies
the life of Jesus may also be revealed.
While we live we are constantly being delivered to
    death for Jesus' sake,
so that the life of Jesus
may be revealed in our mortal flesh.

Paul is rejecting any discouragement or deviation from a courageous ministry for Christ. He sees the Christian apostle as one who is weak and suffering like Christ; but the light of Christ shines on his face and Christ's power works through his weakness.

In the case of Paul, for instance, God first "shines" in his heart. This experience and knowledge of God can produce a like knowledge of God in others. He reveals the light shining on the face of Christ by the light shining from within himself. The weakness of the apostle only proves that all apostolic effectiveness is from God.

In his suffering, Paul seems to compare himself to an animal being pursued in the chase: "pressed upon, but not ferreted out; deprived of a way, but not entirely without escape; pursued, but not headed off; grounded, but not lost utterly" (Nelson Commentary).

This suffering re-enacts the suffering and death of Christ, makes his redemption real among men, but only so that Christ may show, through these weak vessels, how powerful his redemption is.

## 61. Present Suffering Fades in the Light of Eternal Life

2 Cor 4, 13—5, 1
10B-b

We have that spirit of faith
of which the Scripture says,
"Because I believed, I spoke out."
We believe and so we speak,
knowing that he who raised up the Lord Jesus
will raise us up along with Jesus
and place both us and you in his presence.
Indeed, everything is ordered to your benefit
so that the grace bestowed in abundance
may bring greater glory to God
because they who give thanks are many.
We do not lose heart
because our inner being is renewed each day,
even though our body is being destroyed at the same
        time.
The present burden of our trial is light enough
and earns for us an eternal weight of glory
beyond all comparison.
We do not fix our gaze on what is seen
but on what is unseen.
What is seen is transitory;
what is not seen lasts forever.
Indeed, we know that when the earthly tent in which
        we dwell is destroyed
we have a dwelling provided for us by God,
a dwelling in the heavens,
not made by hands, but to last forever.

Paul's body is being gradually given over to death,
either naturally or by the danger of violence from his
enemies. But his "inner man" is constantly being
renewed: not just his soul, but his soul-with-a-right-to-
a-glorious-body-at-the-resurrection. We grow daily in
our inner life with Christ by trying to please the Father
and thus growing more and more like Christ each day.

Compared with what is in store for us—the happiness
of eternal life with God—any and all suffering on earth

is nothing, not worth considering. We have a glimpse or a vision, by the light of faith, of God's final gift to us, and this gives us the courage we need.

Our earthly body—our present "tent" but not our "tomb"—will become an eternally glorious body. We know this with complete certainty. It will be a body that is not the result of natural processes (not built with hands) but still a true and Christlike body.

## 62. Paul's Suffering and Death Are Acts of Worship

2 Tm 4, 6-8. 16-18
30C

I am already being poured out like a libation.
The time of my dissolution is near.
I have fought the good fight,
I have finished the race, I have kept the faith.
From now on a merited crown awaits me;
on that Day the Lord, just judge that he is,
will award it to me—and not only to me
but to all who have looked for his appearing
with eager longing.
At the first hearing of my case in court,
no one took my part.
In fact, everyone abandoned me.
May it not be held against them!
But the Lord stood by my side
and gave me strength,
so that through me the preaching task might be
        completed
and all the nations might hear the gospel.
That is how I was saved from the lion's jaws.
The Lord will continue to rescue me
from all attempts to do me harm
and will bring me safe to his heavenly kingdom.
To him be glory forever and ever. Amen.

Paul expects to be put to death soon. Like the pouring out of wine at sacrifices, the pouring of his blood will be an act of worship to God and a means of salvation for others.

He has confidence because, like Christ, he has "accomplished the work you gave me to do." Like a good athlete, he has fought well in the ring; he has stayed in the race to the end. He has preserved faith for himself and others. Also like a good athlete, he expects the crown of laurel given to winners. The crown here is a symbol of eternal life.

Such statements by Paul are the counterpart of his constant insistence that man is saved by faith alone.

In his arrest Paul was abandoned, like Christ, by all but his Lord. But despite his loneliness and abandonment by friends, he is confident. God rescued him. His first hearing may not have turned out well, but he sees the end, when God will rescue him permanently.

### 63. God's Power and Glory Rest on Paul's Suffering

2 Cor 12, 7-10
14B

As to the extraordinary revelations,
in order that I might not become conceited
I was given a thorn in the flesh,
an angel of Satan to beat me and keep me from getting
      proud.
Three times I begged the Lord that this might leave me.
He said to me, "My grace is enough for you,
for in weakness power reaches perfection."
And so I willingly boast of my weaknesses instead,
that the power of Christ may rest upon me.
Therefore I am content with weakness,

with mistreatment, with distress, with persecutions
and difficulties for the sake of Christ;
for when I am powerless,
it is then that I am strong.

Paul has just spoken of visions and revelations with
which he has been graced. Now, lest he seem to be
boasting unduly, he speaks of his weakness. As one
given extraordinary gifts, he was subject to the temptation of thinking the power was his own.

Therefore God gave him something that counter-
acted the temptation to pride. Paul's "thorn in the
flesh" has always been a mystery to the commentators.
Probably it was a disease or physical infirmity of some
kind (rather than concupiscence or persecution)—chronic,
painful and humiliating.

"I prayed three times" may mean Paul is comparing
himself with Christ in Gethsemane. The tense of the verb
seems to indicate that this kind of prayer has stopped. It
has been "answered" and the "answer" is grace. Grace is
all he needs, and he gets all he needs. Moreover, the all-
sufficiency of God's power must be made evident in
Paul's weakness.

The less one looks to apparent power in man, the
more he sees the real power in God. The weaker the
instrument, the more visible is the skill of the One who
uses the instrument. Christ's power now rests on Paul's
life as God's glory (shekinah) rested on the Temple.

# B. BAPTISM, OUR RISING TO NEW LIFE IN CHRIST

## 64. Putting On Christ in a Totally New Kind of Life

Eph 4, 17. 20-24
18B

I declare and solemnly attest in the Lord
that you must no longer live as the pagans do—
their minds empty.
That is not what you learned
when you learned Christ!
I am supposing, of course,
that he has been preached and taught to you
in accord with the truth that is in Jesus:
namely, that you must lay aside
your former way of life and the old self
which deteriorates through illusion and desire,
and acquire a fresh, spiritual way of thinking.
You must put on that new man
created in God's image,
whose justice and holiness are born of truth.

By God's baptismal consecration we put off our own
selves and our reliance on our own powers ("flesh") and
are radically transformed by putting on Christ. This is
probably a reference to the baptismal ceremony of putting off one's clothing, being plunged into the water,
and coming up out of the water a new person. This
ritual is a sign of divesting oneself of a whole way of
life and putting on *the* new person, Jesus Christ.

This means an end of the "empty-mindedness" that
is characteristic of paganism. Now our minds and hearts
are filled with the One for whom they were made. Vati-

can II says, "By 'the world' is meant the spirit of vanity
and malice which transforms into an instrument of sin
those human energies intended for the service of God
and man."

### 65.  Baptism Is Dying and Rising With Christ

Rom 6, 3-11
13A
Easter Vigil

Are you not aware
that we who were baptized into Christ Jesus
were baptized into his death?
Through baptism into his death
we were buried with him,
so that
just as Christ was raised from the dead
by the glory of the Father,
we too might live a new life.
If we have been united with him
through likeness to his death,
so shall we be through a like resurrection.
This we know:  our old self was crucified with him
so that the sinful body might be destroyed
and we might be slaves to sin no longer.
A man who is dead has been freed from sin.
If we have died with Christ,
we believe that we are also to live with him.
We know that Christ, once raised from the dead,
will never die again;
death has no more power over him.
His death was death to sin, once for all;
his life is life for God.
In the same way,
you must consider yourselves dead to sin
but alive for God in Christ Jesus.

Paul celebrates the freedom Christ won for us, freedom from sin and death. We enter into this new freedom by our Baptism in faith. We are baptized *into* Christ's dying and rising.

Paul's use of *into* may refer to the custom of baptizing by total immersion. Those to be baptized removed their clothing (men and women in separate groups), were anointed with oil, and were dramatically led down into the baptismal pool and immersed beneath the water. They "drowned"; their old self disappeared into the death of Christ and they were "buried" with him. Then they were brought up out of the water, ascended the steps on the other side of the pool, were clothed with a symbolic white garment, and their heads were anointed with oil.

They were raised by the *glory* of the Father, which refers to the power and *showing forth* of God, especially at the Exodus and at Sinai. Just as a flaming *glory* led the Jews to freedom and a new relationship with God, so God's glorious power now continually creates, in Baptism, a new chosen people and a new covenant.

Our life, then, is union with Christ: if we live out our baptismal dying to all that is sinful and selfish, we are being constantly raised up with him to new life. The "sinful body" does not refer to the flesh. Rather, the reference is to the body's mortality (illness, death, or former sin), which is now meaningless, since Baptism has made us Spirit-ual bodies.

Death was "lord"; now Jesus is Lord, having destroyed death—his own and ours. Just as he is totally with his Father in glorious victory, so we are finished with our former sinful life, living a new life centered in Christ, gradually growing more like him.

## 66. Baptism Expresses God's Graciousness in Jesus

Ti 3, 4-7
Christmas, dawn

When the kindness and love of God our Savior
    appeared,
he saved us, not because of any righteous deeds we
    had done,
but because of his mercy.
He saved us through the baptism of new birth
and renewal by the Holy Spirit.
This Spirit he lavished on us
through Jesus Christ our Savior,
that we might be justified by his grace
and become heirs, in hope, of eternal life.

Paul is contrasting a Christian's former life of ignorance, disobedience and enslavement to passion with
the new kind of life that began in Baptism. He has just
exhorted Titus to remind the faithful of their general
duties as Christians: civil obedience, a life of good
deeds, good words, courtesy.

It was all God's doing, this new life. God became
visible as kindness and goodness. Jesus is truly "the
sacrament of the encounter with God." His tender
and generous offer of liberation, life, friendship is
God's grace to us. It is entirely a gift, an absolutely
"gracious" act. Rich and poor, Gentile and Jew, black
and white, are Christians only because God freely
seeks their friendship.

We are born anew and we are new persons in Baptism.
Baptism is the beginning of new life and growth through
the Spirit of the Father and of Jesus, abundantly poured
out on the world. We will inherit eternal life!

### 67. In Baptism Jesus Becomes Our Light

Eph 5, 8-14
4 Lent A

There was a time when you were darkness,
but now you are light in the Lord.
Well, then, live as children of light.
Light produces every kind of goodness
and justice and truth.
Be correct in your judgment
of what pleases the Lord.
Take no part in vain deeds done in darkness;
rather, condemn them.
It is shameful even to mention
the things these people do in secret;
but when such deeds are condemned,
they are seen in the light of day,
and all that then appears is light.
That is why we read:
"Awake, O sleeper,
arise from the dead,
and Christ will give you light."

One of the oldest symbols for sin is darkness; for
a good life, light. Christians' lives are meant to be
illumined and illumining by the light of Christ's life
in them.

Their baptismal rebirth is like God's first creation:
the Spirit hovered over the dark abyss—chaos—and light
was made—beauty and order. Now the Spirit comes into
the Christian, the chaos of sin is destroyed, and the very
light of God shines within. Christ the Light of the world
not only throws light on all that we see; he makes us
bearers of his own light, sacraments to others of God's
love.

The last verses seem to be a fragment of a baptismal
hymn. The risen and exalted Christ awakens us from
death and brings us to life in a new creation.

Pagan and Christian values are as incompatible as
darkness and light. The "deeds of darkness" may refer

to the immorality of some pagan cultic rites. Christian
Baptism, on the other hand, is totally open to the light
and totally filled with the light which produces "every
kind of goodness and justice and truth."

## 68. Forgiveness and Transformation

Col 2, 12-14
17C

In baptism you were not only buried with him
but also raised to life with him
because you believed in the power of God
who raised him from the dead.
Even when you were dead in sin
and your flesh was uncircumcised,
God gave you new life in company with Christ.
He pardoned all our sins.
He canceled the bond that stood against us with all
    its claims,
snatching it up and nailing it to the cross.

The new converts at Colossae were tempted to cling
to some old beliefs—the need to have angels mediate to
God, the divinizing of natural powers, even the observance of the Old Law. Paul insists that the Christian has
died to all that—to sin, to the world, to empty teachings.
In Baptism the Christian is buried with Christ; that is,
he is dead to his former sinful condition, just as Christ
is "dead" to the kind of mortal life he once had. The
Christian is "new" in God's life as Christ is transformed
in the resurrection. This happens through faith in the
power of God.

God forgives before we are sorry. He *is* forgiveness.
We signed an agreement and did not keep it. God can-
celled our debt; he tore up the bill, by nailing it, as it

were, to the cross. Jesus destroyed the debt of all former
law (which forbade sin but could not give the power to
avoid it) by summing up all commandments in his New
Law, the law of the Spirit. In other words, God's life
calls and empowers us beyond all law to love and forgive like Christ himself.

### 69. Newness in the Risen Christ

1 Cor 5, 6-8
Easter

Do you not know that a little yeast
has its effect all through the dough?
Get rid of the old yeast to make of yourselves
fresh dough, unleavened loaves, as it were;
Christ our Passover has been sacrificed.
Let us celebrate the feast not with the old yeast,
that of corruption and wickedness,
but with the unleavened bread
of sincerity and truth.

This selection is read on Easter Sunday, the feast of
baptismal resurrection to new life.

Paul is asking the Church at Corinth to purify itself
by taking disciplinary action against a certain public sinner. The example of yeast refers to a Jewish custom.
Once a year, at Passover, the Jewish housewife got rid
of the yeasted dough she always kept on hand to leaven
new dough. Then she made some altogether new dough
and set it out to acquire new spores of yeast from the
air. In the meantime—during Passover—the family ate
unleavened bread.

The old yeast, in its tastelessness, becomes a meta-
phor for the evil way of life now rejected by the Christian. The use of unleavened bread may also have been a

memorial of the Exodus (a "baptismal" going through water to freedom), when there was no time to let the bread rise.

A little yeast is enough to "corrupt" the whole, yeast being thought of as an unwholesome agent bringing decay. Unleavened bread—uncorrupted—is a symbol of Christian newness of life, a fresh start with the Risen Christ.

Christ is the Passover Lamb, whose blood sets us free through Baptism in faith, just as the blood of lambs, spread on doorposts, was a means of the Jews being saved from death in Egypt and delivered to freedom.


## 70. We Are Children of God

Gal 4, 4-7
January 1

When the designated time had come,
God sent forth his Son born of a woman,
born under the law,
to deliver from the law
those who were subjected to it,
so that we might receive our status as adopted sons.
The proof that you are sons is the fact
that God has sent forth into our hearts
the spirit of his Son
which cries out "Abba!" ("Father!").
You are no longer a slave but a son!
And the fact that you are a son
makes you an heir, by God's design.


Paul is emphasizing the true humanity of Christ. He was born of a woman, a human being, a real mother, in order that he might be our real brother in the flesh, accepting the human condition. Mary is the fully willing means whereby the pre-existent Son could become real man and enter fully into our life, its sorrows, frustrations, human limitations. (This is the only direct mention of Mary in the writings of St. Paul.)

Jesus not only became man, but a *Jewish* man, subject to the Law, and in some way under the "curse" of the Law. Jews had to obey the Law, but it was helpless to save them. Jesus fulfills the Law and replaces it with a new covenant and the Law of the Holy Spirit. Jesus was able to free mankind for a new Father-child relationship.

We are convinced that we are the adopted children of God because we experience within us the presence of the Spirit, who helps us relate to the Father as Jesus did, crying out "Abba!" ("Father!").

### 71. A New, Liberated Existence

Col 3, 1-5. 9-11
18C
Easter

Since you have been raised up
in company with Christ,
set your heart on what pertains to higher realms
where Christ is seated at God's right hand.
Be intent on things above
rather than on things of earth.
After all, you have died!
Your life is hidden now with Christ in God.
When Christ our life appears,
then you shall appear with him in glory.
Put to death whatever in your nature
is rooted in earth: fornication, uncleanness, passion,
evil desires and that lust which is idolatry.
Stop lying to one another.
What you have done is put aside your old self
with its past deeds

89

and put on a new man,
one who grows in knowledge
as he is formed anew in the image of his Creator.
There is no Greek or Jew here,
circumcised or uncircumcised,
foreigner, Scythian, slave, or freeman.
Rather, Christ is everything in all of you.

Christ, risen and victorious, is seated at the right hand
of the Father. By his power, baptismal resurrection has
*already* occurred in Christians; and yet, paradoxically,
it *will* still occur. Christians are called to become what
they already are. Our attitudes and actions should
reflect the new kind of life we have attained in Christ.

The "higher realms" on which we should set our
hearts refer to the transcendent order in which God
acts; not, obviously, to a pre-Copernican heaven "up
there."

In letting our lives be re-oriented in Christ, we reject
the trivial concerns Paul has just reproved—real or apparent slavery to cosmic powers and elemental spirits,
material practices and laws about food and drink, "religious" festivals that do not recognize the fact of our
liberation in Christ. This does not imply a rejection of
the good world God made, but emphasizes a concern
with ultimate values and all that pertains to God's now-
evident will in Christ.

This new order can be attained only by faith. By the
power of Christ's death and resurrection the Christian is
called to die to the selfishness of sin—impurity and anger
are specifically mentioned—and to live a life that is
actually and effectively centered in Christ.

There is a new individual Christian, and there is a new
total Body of Christ. In this new reality there must be
no barriers, whether they are religious (circumcised,
uncircumcised) or social (slave, free man) or racial
(foreigner, Scythian).

## 72. Baptism Is Our Public Profession of Faith

1 Tm 6, 11-16
26C

Man of God that you are,
seek after integrity, piety, faith, love,
steadfastness, and a gentle spirit.
Fight the good fight of faith.
Take firm hold on the everlasting life
to which you were called when,
in the presence of many witnesses,
you made your noble profession of faith.
Before God, who gives life to all,
and before Christ Jesus,
who in bearing witness
made his noble profession before Pontius Pilate,
I charge you to keep God's command
without blame or reproach
until our Lord Jesus Christ shall appear.
This appearance God will bring to pass at his chosen
    time.
He is the blessed and only ruler,
the King of kings and Lord of lords
who alone has immortality
and who dwells in inapproachable light,
whom no human being has ever seen or can see.
To him be honor and everlasting rule! Amen.

In contrast to the money-lovers the author has just
described, he now counsels Timothy to be a responsible
Church leader (though of course "man of God" should
be applied to any Christian). He should seriously "take
hold of" the eternal life he was called to at his great
"profession."

This profession may refer to Timothy's ordination as
a bishop or to an appearance before a tribunal, but
probably it refers to his Baptism in the presence of the
Christian community. His public profession of faith at
that time is likened to that of Jesus before Pontius
Pilate, when he declared himself a king with the mission

to bear witness to the truth. Timothy is to keep God's "command"—Christian truth and/or his own personal faith—until the Second Coming of Jesus.

The last two verses are probably from a hymn. God is Absolute and Eternal King and Lord, immortal and transcendent, beyond human grasp—yet humbly incarnate in the "witness" Jesus.

## C. OUR RISING FOREVER WITH CHRIST

### 73. Our Risen Bodies: What Will They Be Like?

1 Cor 15, 45-49
7C

Scripture has it that Adam, the first man,
became a living soul;
the last Adam has become a life-giving spirit.
Notice the spiritual was not first;
first came the natural and after that the spiritual.
The first man was of earth, formed from dust,
the second is from heaven.
Earthly men are like the man of earth,
heavenly men are like the man of heaven.
Just as we resemble the man from earth,
so shall we bear the likeness
of the man from heaven.

Paul makes this comparison: On earth, our body is en-souled (soul is the principle of our life). After our resurrection, our bodies will be en-Spirited, far beyond what has already been given us on earth. We will be, as body-persons, completely possessed by and docile to the Holy Spirit.

We will be like the risen Christ, the new Adam, who is the source of our spiritual life, just as the first Adam was the source of our mortal life.

All power has come to the totally en-Spirited Christ. As God-man raised to the right hand of the Father, he can send his own Spirit into our hearts and thus make us like himself.

## 74. The Risen Christ Is the Promise That We Too Will Rise

1 Cor 15, 12. 16-20
6C

If Christ is preached as raised from the dead,
how is it that some of you say
there is no resurrection of the dead?
If the dead are not raised,
then Christ was not raised;
and if Christ was not raised,
your faith is worthless.
You are still in your sins,
and those who have fallen asleep in Christ
are the deadest of the dead.
If our hopes in Christ are limited
to this life only,
we are the most pitiable of men.
But as it is,
Christ has been raised from the dead,
the first fruits of those who have fallen asleep.

The Greeks had a certain contempt for the body. Some felt that it was unaffected by salvation. Only the "soul" mattered. This led to two opposite conclusions— one justifying bodily immorality (it didn't count) and the other demanding great mortification. Paul contradicts both by his defense of the resurrection.

If, as his opponents say, our bodies cannot rise, then the resurrection of Jesus—also a true man—was also impossible. Likewise our whole faith is without foundation; our sins are not forgiven; the dead have totally perished.

But, in fact, we will rise because we are incorporated—"embodied"—into Christ. We share his risen life *now*; the *final* fruit of redemption will be our resurrection.

The *first* fruit of redemption is the risen Christ. First fruits were offered as a symbol of the dedication of the whole harvest (Nm 15, 18). So the resurrection of Christ is the promise and sign of later fruits—our resurrection. Christ rose from the dead at just about the time of the year when the sheaf of first fruits was offered.

### 75. Christ Will Transfigure Our Bodies to His Likeness

Phil 3, 17–4, 1
2 Lent C

Be imitators of me, my brothers.
Take as your guide those who follow the example that
    we set.
Unfortunately, many go about in a way
which shows them to be enemies
of the cross of Christ.
I have often said this to you before;
this time I say it with tears.
Such as these will end in disaster!
Their god is their belly
and their glory is in their shame.
I am talking about those who are set upon the things
    of this world.
[As you well know,
we have our citizenship in heaven;
it is from there that we eagerly await
the coming of our savior, the Lord Jesus Christ.

He will give a new form
to this lowly body of ours
and remake it according to the pattern of his glorified
    body,
by his power to subject everything to himself.]
For these reasons, my brothers,
you whom I so love and long for,
you who are my joy and my crown,    '
continue, my dear ones,
to stand firm in the Lord.

Christ will come and make our bodies like his glorious
body, and we will finally and fully experience the power
and freedom of divine life. Note that Paul does not call
this an "escape" from the body.

Without neglecting the world, we cannot confine our
interests to this earth. We are, in a sense, already citizens
of heaven. Paul therefore asks the Philippians to imitate
*him* in contrast to those who deny the spirit of sacrifice
and the meaning of the cross and who are dominated by
this-worldly concerns that corrupt religious faith.

Paul rejects both extremes mentioned above: the
libertinism which does not restrain physical appetites—
as if a purely "spiritual" God didn't care; and those who
make their "belly" (that is, dietary laws) their god. They
glory in their "shame" (that is, circumcision), instead of
the cross. Both those groups are enemies of the cross,
though they profess to accept it.

## 76. Our Resurrection:
## A Christian Hymn of Victory Over Death

1 Cor 15, 54-58
8C

When the corruptible frame takes on incorruptibility
and the mortal immortality,

then will the saying of Scripture be fulfilled:
"Death is swallowed up in victory."
"O death, where is your victory?
O death, where is your sting?"
The sting of death is sin,
and sin gets its power from the law.
But thanks be to God who has given us the victory
through our Lord Jesus Christ.
Be steadfast and persevering, my beloved brothers,
fully engaged in the work of the Lord.
You know that your toil is not in vain
when it is done in the Lord.

The resurrection of the dead is the final evidence of Christ's victory. Paul turns around a saying from Hosea. The prophet has God looking for something with which to punish Israel for its sins. God supposedly asks, "Where is your sting, O nether world?"—so that God can use it against Israel. But now, after Jesus' resurrection, the question becomes a taunt at the powerlessness of death. "Where is your sting *now*, Death? It's destroyed!" Like a poisonous serpent, death has been "de-fanged," deprived of its power to kill.

Death is seen here almost as a personified enemy of man, using sin to destroy him. But at the resurrection death will have been vanquished, as we share in Jesus' victory over death.

Paul sees the Law, now fulfilled in Christ, as a power of sin. Although the Law demands obedience, it does not provide the power to obey. Therefore, when disobeyed, it makes sin manifest, and thus in a sense increases sin and makes it more powerful.

Paul now hopes he has quieted the fears of the Corinthians: they *will* rise. Therefore the "hard work" of the Christian life is not in vain because they live in the victorious Christ. They should try to make constant progress in Christian virtue, drawn on by the knowledge of the glorious destiny awaiting them.

## 77. Heaven: We Shall Be With the Lord Unceasingly

1 Thes 4, 13-17
32A

We would have you be clear
about those who sleep in death, brothers;
otherwise you might yield to grief
like those who have no hope.
For if we believe that Jesus died and rose,
God will bring forth with him from the dead
those also who have fallen asleep believing in him.
We say to you, as if the Lord himself had said it,
that we who live, who survive until his coming,
will in no way have an advantage
over those who have fallen asleep.
No, the Lord himself will come down from heaven
at the word of command,
at the sound of the archangel's voice and God's trumpet;
and those who have died in Christ will rise first.
Then we, the living, the survivors,
will be caught up with them in the clouds
to meet the Lord in the air.
Thenceforth we shall be with the Lord unceasingly.
Console one another with this message.

Paul's people in Thessalonia were not worried about whether or not the Christian dead would rise to glory with Christ; they were worried the dead would miss the great joy of the actual coming of Christ and join the celebration only *later*.

Paul reassures them that the dead will indeed share in the glorious coming. In fact, their resurrection will be the first phase of the celebration.

In any case, they are not to grieve for the dead with a *pagan* sorrow—one that has no hope. The Christian dead are merely asleep. They were united to Christ on earth, and still are. At the final coming they will be fully united.

Paul apparently had some hope that he would be alive at the coming of Christ—though he insists (5, 1) that no one knows the day. He now uses apocalyptic language (used in both Old and New Testaments) to describe that day. The details need not be taken literally for example, that (heaven is "up there" from whence Christ will come and that we will have to go "up" to meet him). We will be caught up in the clouds—the traditional veil over God and Christ.

The point is, then, that all Christians who believe in Christ will be mysteriously transformed. Their bodies will be made incorruptible and immortal. They will enjoy the vision and union with God forever.

## D. EUCHARISTIC WORSHIP

### 78. The Eucharist, Saving Sacrifice and Covenant

1 Cor 11, 23-26
Holy Thursday
Corpus Christi C

I received from the Lord what I handed on to you,
namely, that the Lord Jesus
on the night in which he was betrayed took bread,
and after he had given thanks, broke it and said,
"This is my body, which is for you.
Do this in remembrance of me."
In the same way, after the supper, he took the cup,
saying,
"This cup is the new covenant in my blood.
Do this, whenever you drink it, in remembrance of me."
Every time, then, you eat this bread and drink this cup,
you proclaim the death of the Lord until he comes!

Paul has been reprimanding the Corinthians for their conduct during the agape and Eucharist. It is an insult to the sacredness of the occasion. To impress them with the seriousness and solemnity of the Eucharist, he

recalls what he has "handed on" to them after learning
it from the primitive Christian community.

It is a sacrifice of *salvation*: "This is my body which
is *for you*." We eat the Eucharistic bread, as the Jews ate
the Paschal Lamb, to commemorate God's saving action:
*then* from slavery in Egypt; *now* from slavery to sin,
Satan and death.

The former covenant was sealed by blood, the sign of
life and therefore the sign of the union of our life with
God. Now Christ's blood poured out seals the new covenant, and each Eucharist renews that covenant.

In the Eucharist we "proclaim" the death of Christ—
that is, we proclaim that he has redeemed us by his death
and resurrection—and we enter into that redemption. It
is a sign, or sacrament, "until he comes."

This statement of Paul is the earliest written testimony
(about 57 A.D.) about the Eucharist.

### 79. The Sacrament of Loving Unity

1 Cor 10, 16-17
Corpus Christi A

Is not the cup of blessing we bless
a sharing in the blood of Christ?
And is not the bread we break
a sharing in the body of Christ?
Because the loaf of bread is one, we, many though we
    are,
are one body for we all partake of the one loaf.

Paul has been dissuading the Corinthians from partici-
pation in idol worship because it makes them *sharers*
with the demons. Conversely, participating in the Eucharist actually makes them *sharers* in Christ.

The Eucharist is the sacrament of unity. This is not a

mere physical or legal unity, but the wholehearted unity
of love between God and his children and amongst the
children themselves. The Eucharist unites the Christian
with Christ and in a special way with his fellow Christians.

We actually share in the body and blood of the living
Christ. We are thus brought to achieve what Jesus came
for: "that they may be one." The one *loaf* makes us
one, rather than *our* joining together to "make" the
Body of Christ. The loaf is one; all who receive the one
Christ with faith and love become one with him and
with all who receive him. The Eucharist is the sign of an
already existing unity and the cause of greater unity.

## 80. The Living Sacrifice of Our Selves

Rom 12, 1-2
22A

Brothers, I beg you through the mercy of God
to offer your bodies as a living sacrifice
holy and acceptable to God, your spiritual worship.
Do not conform yourselves to this age,
but be transformed by the renewal of your mind,
so that you may judge what is God's will,
what is good, pleasing and perfect.

The mercy of God calls for self-giving on our part.
We are no longer asked, as were the people of the Old
Covenant, to offer cultic animal sacrifices to express
our thanks and adoration. With the full revelation of
God in Jesus, we are called to give our very life as he did.
The life of a Christian has been made holy. It is worthy
to be a spiritual offering.

"Offer your bodies," considering Paul's overall viewpoint, means "offer your persons. Put your whole lives

into the hands of God, for his service." Our self-sacrifice is a living one, and a "spiritual" one—that is, guided by reason and also intangible, internal, not merely "out there."

Our commitment occurs when God changes us. (The passive "be transformed" suggests that God is the agent.) He takes us from a self-centered, shallow viewpoint to an attitude that sees his will in all situations. The Christian attitude can discern good in the midst of what is bad (the "fleshly" world). He can discern what is pleasing to God but not necessarily to men, as well as what is "perfect,"—that is, what achieves its God-given purpose.

### 81. Eternal Glory to God, Through Christ

Rom 16, 25-27
4 Advent B

To him who is able to strengthen you in the gospel
which I proclaim when I preach Jesus Christ,
the gospel which reveals the mystery hidden for many
    ages
but now manifested through the writings of the
    prophets,
and, at the command of the eternal God,
made known to all the Gentiles
that they may believe and obey—
to him, the God who alone is wise,
may glory be given through Jesus Christ unto endless
    ages. Amen.

This is the end of Paul's letter to the Romans and another reminder of the "end" of all Christian life, the giving of glory to God, through Christ. The very purpose of the Incarnation is to make it possible for man to glorify God in a fitting way, with the love of the Spirit, in Jesus.

God alone is the Good News, the wisdom and love that our heart and mind instinctively seek. In him and for him everything lives and moves and has its being.

Though it is almost blasphemous to say it, let us be clear: God's making human beings for his own glory is not the act of one who is greedy for praise. It is simply the only plan God could have had. God alone is goodness, happiness, love. To glorify God is to be thrilled at this reality, to open ourselves to it, to be so totally absorbed that we forget ourselves. In so doing, even without trying, we find ourselves; and we also find more happiness than the greatest greed could desire.

In the Eucharist we give glory to God through Christ.

## 82. All for the Glory of God

1 Cor 10, 31–11, 1
6B

Whether you eat or drink—whatever you do—
you should do all for the glory of God.
Give no offense to Jew or Greek or to the church of
    God,
just as I try to please all in any way I can
by seeking not my own advantage,
but that of the many that they may be saved.
Imitate me as I imitate Christ.

Again, the purpose of life is to give God glory. Our Christian lives are summed up when we go with Jesus to the Father in Eucharistic sacrifice.

Paul has been discussing the question of conscience of both "weak" and "strong" persons with regard to the eating of meat once offered to idols. The highest principle of all is invoked: "Do all for the glory of God." This avoids legalism and human respect on the one hand, and a reckless independence on the other.

He concludes with a reminder of the effect of Christian conduct on others both inside and outside the Church. Whatever their conscience decides (about the eating of the meat), they must not put stumbling blocks in the way of the conversion of Jew or Gentile.

Again Paul shows a healthy self-confidence: He is a good example to them. He has renounced salary and privileges and sought only one thing, the salvation of men for the glory of God.

## E. FAITH

### 83. We Come to Holiness Only by the Gift of Faith

Rom 3, 21-25.28
9A

Now the justice of God
has been manifested apart from the law,
even though both law and prophets bear witness to it—
that justice of God which works through faith in
    Jesus Christ
for all who believe.
All men have sinned
and hence are deprived of the glory of God.
All men are now undeservedly justified by the gift
    of God,
through the redemption wrought in Christ Jesus.
Through his blood,
God made him the means of expiation for all who
    believe.
For we hold that a man is justified by faith
apart from observance of the law.

*Now*, as compared with the time when there was only the Law, which laid down obligations but offered no power to observe them; *now*, God has given us a new and gracious way of being saved. We need only consent in order to make his mercy our own. And we consent by believing wholeheartedly in Christ the Savior. This is faith.

Here the "justice" of God does not refer to punishment but to his saving mercy, whereby he delivers his people through an act resembling acquittal. Man is "justified," (that is, made holy with God's own "justice") by responding in faith—a conscious, deliberate and free act, made possible by God's gift. We admit our insufficiency and submit ourselves totally to the love of God.

All mankind is in sin, deprived of the "glory" of God, that is, of the "justice" of God as it was meant to be shared by mankind (sanctifying grace, eternal life). We are freely justified by God's gift through Christ. Holiness is due *only* to the benevolence of God; no human act prior to justification can cause it.

Redemption has been wrought in Jesus. In principle, and objectively, the whole world has been saved. In liberating Christ from death and welcoming him to his heavenly home, God received all men and offered *them* full pardon and peace.

On the Day of Atonement the high priest entered the Holy of Holies and sprinkled blood on the golden plate over the ark, called the Propitiatory. It was the plate where God was believed to be enthroned. Blood meant life, and therefore union with God's life. Paul says Jesus is the real Propitiatory. His own blood was sprinkled upon himself—surely the "place" where God was—and the deadness of man was made alive again with the life of God. Here "expiation" and "propitiation" mean prayer which depends for its value on the interior value of the worshipers. Essentially it is a recalling of God's promises, and thus becomes an act of faith in God's faithfulness.

Luther added a word here: "justified by faith *alone*."
Trent condemned not the expression but the interpretation, namely, that all other works except faith are worthless both before and after justification. Paul is concerned here only with the way of *obtaining* justification. No one can earn it by works according to this or that system of law—whether Jewish or Gentile, whether natural law, ceremonial law or moral law.

Paul leaves no doubt that works are necessary to *retain* the justification obtained by faith (cf. Rom 12—14; 1 Cor 3, 8; Gal 5, 6). But he would call these "works of faith," not "works of law." "Faith leads to virtue, but virtue does not lead to faith" (St. Gregory).

### 84. The Response God Awakens in Our Hearts

Eph 1, [15-16], 17-20
Ascension
2nd Sunday of Christmas

[For my part,
from the first time I heard of your faith in the Lord
     Jesus
and your love for all members of the church,
I have never stopped thanking God for you
and recommending you in my prayers.]
May the God of our Lord Jesus Christ, the Father of
     glory,
grant you a spirit of wisdom and insight
to know him clearly.
May he enlighten your innermost vision
that you may know the great hope to which he called
     you,
the wealth of his glorious heritage
to be distributed among the members of the church
and the immeasurable scope of his power in us who
     believe.

It is like the strength he showed
in raising Christ from the dead.

Faith must love. Faith is the gift of giving ourselves
totally to the Father in Christ. We thereby appreciate
the love the Father shows us, and we express this appreciation by our love of others.

Paul prays that our love of God not be intellectual
only, but an *experiencing* of his great love, an enlight-
ening of our heart whereby we "see" the inheritance
that will be ours.

Faith is a transforming encounter with God, a personal sense of God's love for us. In this transforming
experience, we will realize the true nature of the *hope*
we are called to have, the precious *treasure* we will
inherit, and the *power* of God present in us. This power
available to us is nothing less than the divine power
the Father showed in raising Jesus from the dead.

### 85. God Alone Creates Faith in Us

1 Cor 2, 1-5
5A

As for myself, brothers, when I came to you
I did not come proclaiming God's testimony
with any particular eloquence or "wisdom."
No, I determined that while I was with you
I would speak of nothing but Jesus Christ and him
     crucified.
When I came among you it was in weakness and fear,
and with much trepidation.
My message and my preaching
had none of the persuasive force of "wise"
     argumentation,
but the convincing power of the Spirit.
As a consequence,

your faith rests not on the wisdom of men
but on the power of God.

Paul is emphasizing the fact that faith is entirely a
gift instilled by the Spirit. It cannot be humanly "pro-
duced" by reasoning or rhetoric or Greek wisdom
(*sophia*).

Paul presents Jesus as "weak" (that is, crucified); our
faith is not dependent on "strong" arguments that over-
whelm by their length or learnedness. Paul simply presents what amounted to *God's own testimony* about
Jesus: the resurrection.

Paul is not being anti-intellectual (there was "instruction" in the Church after the simple proclamation of
the Good News) or simplistic. He is attacking excessive
self-confidence in a "fleshly" human reason as a self-
sufficient means of salvation.

Paul also stresses his own weakness shared with
Christ. He came to Corinth (after his failure in Athens)
"weak, nervous and shaking with fear." The real
strength lies in the message, not the messenger; in the
word and power of the Spirit, not in human wisdom.

Hence real faith is entirely God's creation, instilled
by the Spirit. Paul proclaims the Good News: Jesus—
crucified and risen. God creates faith in us through this
proclamation.

## 86. God Makes Us Holy by Our Gift of Faith

Rom 4, 18-25
10A

Abraham believed hoping against hope,
and so became the father of many nations,
just as it was once told him,
"Numerous as this shall your descendants be."

Without growing weak in faith he thought of his
    own body,
which was as good as dead
(for he was nearly a hundred years old)
and of the dead womb of Sarah.
Yet he never questioned or doubted God's promise;
rather, he was strengthened in faith and gave glory to
    God,
fully persuaded that God could do whatever he had
    promised.
Thus his faith was credited to him as justice.

Abraham's justification is proof that our justification
is by faith and not by works. Abraham's faith was such
that he believed God's promise even when appearances
indicated he could never be the father of a son and of
many nations. He seemed past the age of fatherhood
and Sarah's womb was "lifeless." Later, God asked him
to sacrifice his son Isaac. Abraham simply believed God.

Some Jews thought Abraham's being chosen was a
reward for being a just man. Paul contradicts them:
God is simply faithful to his promises. His act of justifying is unilateral, free, unmerited.

God's "justice" is his saving mercy. It is primarily
concerned with vindicating the innocent and the poor.
Man's "justice" participates in the justice (righteousness)
of God; it is a sharing in God's holiness. It is "right" and
"just" for God to love us, because he has made us lova-
ble.

Our "justice" is finally a sharing in the life of the
risen Christ. Because of his death and resurrection, he
gives life to all by communicating his Spirit. Our faith is
true faith if, like Abraham, we believe God unquestion-
ingly.

## 87. By Faith We Have Been Crucified With Christ and Now Live With Him

Gal 2, 16. 19-21
11C

Knowing that a man is not justified by legal observance
but by faith in Jesus Christ,
we too have believed in him
in order to be justified by faith in Christ,
not by observance of the law;
for by works of the law no one will be justified.
It was through the law that I died to the law,
to live for God.
I have been crucified with Christ,
and the life I live now is not my own;
Christ is living in me.
I still live my human life,
but it is a life of faith in the Son of God,
who loved me and gave himself for me.
I will not treat God's gracious gift as pointless.
If justice is available through the law,
then Christ died to no purpose!

God makes us "just" (upright, holy) by changing us
internally, so that we lead a new life of living union with
Christ. Paul insists that this does not happen through
obeying the Mosaic Law (and/or its Pharisaic interpretation), but through faith in Christ Jesus—that is, the attitude whereby we accept God's self-revelation in Jesus
and respond with a complete dedication of life to him.

By "justification" Paul means an interior purification
whereby our sins are utterly blotted out and we are
made acceptable to God in virtue of faith which shows
itself in charity.

"With Christ I am 'co-crucified,' " Paul says. The
Christian is another Christ in virtue of a mystical union
with him. This union has been made possible by the
crucifixion, but can be said to be remotely caused by
the Law: Christ died because the curse of the Law was
laid on him (Gal 3, 13)—that is, he took upon himself

the curse of man's sin. Thus Paul is able to say that "it was through the Law that I died to the Law."

We live by faith in the Son of God. Christ lives in us and remakes us in our very being, giving us a new principle of life. He is not merely present psychologically. But his renewal of our being should penetrate into our psychological awareness so that we *realize* in faith that our real life comes from him. Through faith and Baptism we have been identified with Christ's passion, death and resurrection so that we can live for God.

### 88. Faith Is in Our Hearts and on Our Lips

Rom 10, 8-13
1 Lent C

What does Scripture say?
"The word is near you, on your lips and in your heart
(that is, the word of faith which we preach)."
For if you confess with your lips that Jesus is Lord,
and believe in your heart
that God raised him from the dead,
you will be saved.
Faith in the heart leads to justification,
confession on the lips to salvation.
Scripture says, "No one who believes in him
will be put to shame."
Here there is no difference between Jew and Greek;
all have the same Lord,
rich in mercy toward all who call upon him.
"Everyone who calls on the name of the Lord
will be saved."

Paul's point is this: Whereas in the old Jewish view it was difficult to "attain" holiness because of the great moral effort required, in the new covenant it is "easy" because it is a gift. The faith we have received is near and easy—on our very lips and in our heart. The risen Jesus is Lord.

Paul is not contrasting lips and heart. Faith is present in the heart before it is professed, and the external manifestation of faith makes it fully human, for we are flesh/spirit persons.

A similar Semitic parallelism (not contrast) exists regarding justification and salvation: Both are on our lips, both are in our heart—by faith.

Faith is God's offer to everyone. Both Jews and Gentiles are equally undeserving of the gift; but both are equally recipients of God's generosity.

### 89. We Move Confidently to Judgment Through Our Time of Faith

2 Cor 5, 6-10
11B

We continue to be confident.
We know that while we dwell in the body we are away
    from the Lord.
We walk by faith, not by sight.
I repeat, we are full of confidence,
and would much rather be away from the body
and at home with the Lord.
This being so, we make it our aim to please him
whether we are with him or away from him.
The lives of all of us are to be revealed
before the tribunal of Christ
so that each one may receive his recompense,
good or bad,
according to his life in the body.

During this time of faith we are not yet definitively united to God, but we are sure of that final blessing by

111

our firm Christian hope. If we have a true view of the meaning of death—meeting God in Christ and in his Spirit—we may even desire death, but the normal shrinking from the separation of body and soul would also usually be present. Whether we live or die, our purpose is the same: to please the Father.

The last verses express the Christian belief in the possession of eternal happiness following judgment.

### 90. The Wisdom of Mature Christians

1 Cor 2, 6-10
6A

There is, to be sure, a certain wisdom which we express
      among the spiritually mature.
It is not a wisdom of this age, however,
nor of the rulers of this age who are men headed for
      destruction.
No, what we utter is God's wisdom:
a mysterious, a hidden wisdom.
God planned it before all ages for our glory.
None of the rulers of this age knew the mystery;
if they had known it,
they would never have crucified the Lord of glory.
Of this wisdom it is written:
"Eye has not seen, ear has not heard,
nor has it so much as dawned on man
what God has prepared for those who love him."
Yet God has revealed this wisdom to us through the
      Spirit.
The Spirit scrutinizes all matters, even the deep things
      of God.

Christ is the Wisdom of God, the gift given us by the Spirit. Faith possesses this Wisdom.

The "perfect" Christians have a much deeper understanding of the mystery-Christ. They are fully grown in him, spiritually mature Christians. By contrast, those who are spiritually "infants" have indeed received the Spirit in Baptism but still think and act in a "fleshly" way. They are still too attached to the unredeemed "world."

"This age" or "world" is that part of mankind which has sinfully refused to accept Christ. They allow themselves to be enslaved by Satan and the evil powers.

Mature persons are also the "spiritual" persons who are completely docile to the Spirit, whereas "material" Christians have scarcely risen above a merely natural way of thinking and acting.

Christ is a mystery who can be known only by God's revealing himself. He is Wisdom hidden in the foolishness of the Cross. If the evil powers had known who he was, they would not have destroyed themselves by crucifying him. Note that Christ is both Messiah and Lord God (the word for Yahweh).

"Eye hath not seen . . ." refers to the mystery of Christ hidden in God from eternity. Such an impossible dream would never have dawned on the mind of man— that God would become man.

## 91. Faith, Hope, Charity— God's Gift and Our Response

1 Thes 1, 1-5
29A

Paul, Silvanus, and Timothy,
to the church of Thessalonians
who belong to God the Father and the Lord Jesus
    Christ.
Grace and peace be yours.
We keep thanking God for all of you

and we remember you in our prayers,
for we constantly are mindful before our God and
     Father
of the way you are proving your faith,
and laboring in love,
and showing constancy in hope in our Lord Jesus
     Christ.
We know, too, brothers beloved of God, how you
     were chosen.
Our preaching of the gospel
proved not a mere matter of words for you
but one of power;
it was carried on in the Holy Spirit and out of complete
     conviction.

This is the beginning of the First Letter to the Thessalonians, written around 51 A.D. It is probably Paul's first epistle and the first of all New Testament writings. He wants to give joy and encouragement to his converts in the city from which he was driven by unbelievers.

Paul praises the *work* of their faith—total personal commitment to God as revealed in Christ; the *endurance* of their hope—patient expectation of salvation while suffering; and the labor, the *hard work* of their charity. God authors these virtues and is their ultimate object. But they are also man's response to God, and they actively mobilize the Christian to work and labor and endure.

Proof of God's loving power is seen in the effectiveness of Paul's preaching to the Thessalonians, in the work of the Spirit, and in their sincerity.

## F. 'AS WE WAIT IN JOYFUL HOPE'

### 92. Now Is the Hour of Salvation

Rom 13, 11-14
1 Advent A

You know the time in which we are living.
It is now the hour for you to wake from sleep,
for our salvation is closer
than when we first accepted the faith.
The night is far spent; the day draws near.
Let us cast off deeds of darkness
and put on the armor of light.
Let us live honorably as in daylight;
not in carousing and drunkenness,
not in sexual excess and lust,
not in quarreling and jealousy.
Rather, put on the Lord Jesus Christ
and make no provision for the desires of the flesh.

Paul says, "Wake up! It is the new day! Put on Jesus!"
He has just reviewed his favorite theme, charity, the true
fulfillment of all law. He now suggests another reason
for love—readiness for the moment of salvation *which is
always unfolding.*

*Now* is the time of Christ, the hour of salvation,
because the risen Christ has brought the "day" of living
honorably. Faith is waking up eagerly to meet a new
day; the sunshine is Christ.

The "hour" of salvation began with the death and
resurrection of Christ. Now is the time set aside for the
conversion of mankind. Each moment now promises
the eternity of God's life. Now is always the appropriate

time to make our own the salvation offered in Christ.

The night and darkness of evil living are past for the Christian. He has put on new "armor"—Jesus himself. By Baptism he has done this in principle; now—always now—we are to live out this identification more and more by rejecting evil desires and growing in charity. We need a psychological deepening of what has happened to our being.

### 93. Alertness in Waiting for Christ

1 Thes 5, 1-6
33A

As regards specific times and moments, brothers,
we do not need to write you;
you know very well that the day of the Lord
is coming like a thief in the night.
Just when people are saying, "Peace and security,"
ruin will fall on them
with the suddenness of pains overtaking a woman in
    labor,
and there will be no escape.
You are not in the dark, brothers,
that the day might catch you off guard, like a thief.
No, all of you are children of light and of the day.
We belong neither to darkness nor to night;
therefore let us not be asleep like the rest, but awake
    and sober!

"The Day of the Lord," in earliest times, meant God's special intervention. Through it his power triumphed in people. In Amos 5, 18-20 we have the first instance of its meaning a day of punishment for sinners. During the Exile it meant a time when God would avenge Israel against her oppressors and bring about her restoration. Finally it came to mean the day of final judgment, the

Second Coming, the *parousia*.

It will come suddenly and unexpectedly, like a thief in the night. We must not expect to be prepared by spectacular signs. It is inescapable. The efforts of everybody come under the scrutiny of Truth.

Paul repeats Jesus' warning against being complacent: We ought to be ready for his coming at any time. He also repeats Jesus' words about when this will occur: "The exact time is not yours to know. The Father has reserved that to himself" (Acts 1, 7).

Christians are people who have been filled with the Light. They are "daytime" people, awake and alert. They reject the stupor and misery of darkness, the symbol of sin.

Christians are alert for Christ's coming as lovers are eager for reunion. Jesus says, "The man who hears my word and has faith in him who sent me possesses eternal life. He does not come under condemnation" (Jn 5, 24).

### 94. The Coming of Christ Must Be Uppermost in Our Minds

1 Cor 7, 29-31
3B

I tell you, brothers, the time is short.
From now on those with wives should live as though
     they had none;
those who weep should live as though they were not
     weeping,
and those who rejoice as though they were not rejoicing;
buyers should conduct themselves as though they
     owned nothing,
and those who make use of the world as though they
     were not using it,
for the world as we know it is passing away.

Paul suggests a change of attitude toward all earthly things. This world is not final—it is rushing toward its consummation. Christians ought not to be over-influenced by fleeting and perishable things, remembering that everything is passing away. The "last days," the period of God's definitive salvation, began with the death and resurrection of Christ.

Detachment means making a proper preparation for the coming of the Lord. Everything—cares, feelings, activities, even the fulfillment of the marriage vocation—is secondary (but not contradictory) to the spirit of faith and watchfulness.

Paul has been speaking of voluntarily chosen virginity. He sees the unmarried man and woman as free to devote themselves entirely to God's service, whereas the married person can find it difficult to give undivided attention to Christ. But Paul has no intention of forcing this upon anyone, or casting aspersions on marriage. He is saying: The Last Day is here; let this fact be the primary influence in your life.

### 95. Avoiding Anxiety About the Coming

2 Thes 1, 11—2, 2
31C

We pray for you always
that our God may make you worthy of his call,
and fulfill by his power
every honest intention and work of faith.
In this way the name of our Lord Jesus
may be glorified in you and you in him,
in accord with the gracious gift of our God
and of the Lord Jesus Christ.
On the question of the coming of our Lord Jesus Christ
and our being gathered to him,

we beg you, brothers,
not to be so easily agitated or terrified,
whether by an oracular utterance or rumor
or a letter alleged to be ours,
into believing that the day of the Lord is here.

Paul is answering two questions: a) What about the gathering of the faithful to Christ at his coming? This is a reference to the final gathering of Israel from the Dispersion, now applied to Christians. b) Is it true that the *parousia* has already come? Paul's use of apocalyptic imagery is difficult to follow.

He says that because of a) a false "gift" of prophecy, b) a misunderstanding of Paul's letter, or c) a forged letter, some have held that the Second Coming has already happened.

Some Christians seemed to have held that salvation was totally complete and was enjoyed now in the sacramental life. Paul denies this because it would restrict the Lordship of Jesus who must triumph over *all* evil and resistance to God. Full salvation will come only when the cosmos and all history is redeemed and God's kingship fulfilled. This is still in the future.

There will be a final "assembly" of the people of God and a glorious coming of Christ. But it is not, in fact, "dawning." The Thessalonians have become upset and terrified about this matter, and Paul begs them to calm down.

Paul's prayer delicately puts in perspective both man's effort ("honest intention and work of faith") and God's all-embracing grace making man worthy and fulfilling his resolves. Jesus and the Church are glorified in each other, always through the grace-gift-love of God.

## 96. Meanwhile, the Work of This Life

2 Thes 2, 7-12
33C

You know how you ought to imitate us.
We did not live lives of disorder when we were among
    you,
nor depend on anyone for food.
Rather, we worked day and night,
laboring to the point of exhaustion so as not to impose
    on any of you.
Not that we had no claim on you,
but that we might present ourselves as an example for
    you to imitate.
Indeed, when we were with you we used to lay down
    the rule
that anyone who would not work should not eat.
We hear that some of you are unruly,
not keeping busy but acting like busybodies.
We enjoin all such,
and we urge them strongly in the Lord Jesus Christ
to earn the food they eat by working quietly.

While concerning himself with the final coming of
Christ, Paul's main intention is to encourage the Christians of Thessalonia to persevere during their time of
trouble. God will reward courage and patience in persecution.

Some, however, felt that this final vindication was so
near that there was no point in continuing daily work.
It was useless.

Paul calls this "disorderliness." They are depending
on others for food when they could be providing their
own. There is a pun in the Greek that may be expressed
by saying that they were "not busy, but busybodies."
The rule should be, "No work, no food." Paul offers
himself and his tent-making work as an example for
them. There is still need to work.

Christians are to engage fully in earthly tasks, no
matter how near or far the final coming is. Each should

support himself according to his ability, working quietly and steadily, always in readiness for the Lord.

### 97. Peace and Joy: Christ Is Always Near

Phil 4, 4-7
3 Advent C

Rejoice in the Lord always! I say it again. Rejoice!
Everyone should see how unselfish you are.
The Lord himself is near. Dismiss all anxiety from
    your minds.
Present your needs to God in every form of prayer and
    in petitions full of gratitude.
Then God's own peace,
which is beyond all understanding,
will stand guard over your hearts and minds,
in Christ Jesus.

The Lord is near. In time? In space? In grace? In power? Paul at one time in his life felt that he would see the final coming of Jesus. But even so, the important fact is that Christ's certain coming should affect our lives at all times, whether his "final" coming occurs today or 20 years from now.

Christ is always coming, always near, always here. He is therefore always a source of *joy*—a corrective to the childish notion that his coming should be an ordeal.

Likewise, Christ's ever-coming affects our prayer. Our petitions are joyful, confident, always coupled with gratitude, because we know that our loving Father "answers" us before we ask, with more than we could possibly want.

## 98. Waiting for Christ:  Progress in Holiness

1 Thes 3, 12—4, 2
1 Advent C

May the Lord increase you
and make you overflow with love for one another and
     for all,
even as our love does for you.
May he strengthen your hearts,
making them blameless and holy before our God and
     Father
at the coming of our Lord Jesus with all his holy ones.
Now, my brothers, we beg and exhort you in the Lord
     Jesus
that, even as you learned from us how to conduct
     yourselves in a way pleasing to God—
which you are indeed doing—
so you must learn to make still greater progress.
You know the instructions we gave you in the Lord
     Jesus.

The Christian life is to be "ready," blameless and
holy—for the coming of Jesus.

This is not the defensive readiness of those who
merely don't want to be caught in sin or who merely
want to make sure that God "has nothing on them."
It is rather a life wherein God constantly "increases"
*us*, as persons, and makes us *overflow* with love for each
other. This is our first concern. If we open ourselves to
this gracious plan of God, we are "automatically" ready
for his coming at any time.

Still, there is no once-and-for-all readiness. Life is
growth. Paul praises the people of the Thessalonian
community for learning to conduct themselves in a way
pleasing to God. But he appeals to them to *progress*—to
open themselves more completely to the call of God in
all situations, to let God deepen and enrich his relationship with them. The inspiration:  all we have learned in
the Lord Jesus.

An additional motive:  The Jesus we await will come

"with his holy ones"—probably all Christians, living and dead. What a great inspiration to have the privilege of belonging to that great community.

### 99.  How Great the Harvest of Holiness Will Be

Phil 1, 4-6. 8-11
2 Advent C

In every prayer I utter, I rejoice as I plead on your
    behalf,
at the way you have all continually helped promote
    the gospel from the very first day.
I am sure of this much:
that he who has begun the good work in you will carry
    it through to completion,
right up to the day of Christ Jesus.
God himself can testify how much I long for each of
    you with the affection of Christ Jesus!
My prayer is that your love may more and more
    abound,
both in understanding and wealth of experience,
so that with a clear conscience and blameless conduct
you may learn to value the things that really matter,
up to the very day of Christ. It is my wish that you may
    be found rich in the harvest of justice
which Jesus Christ has ripened in you,
to the glory and praise of God.

God has "planted" holiness in the Church at Philippi. It was and is his initiative, always his gift. And the same good God will *ripen* this holiness right up to the day Christ comes again. What God begins, he finishes.

Now, if our life this far has been so good, who can imagine what the future will bring? Who knows what the "harvest" of holiness will be? Paul prays that we may trust in the divine greatness of our life, the hidden harvest quietly growing.

What is this life God gives? It is a life of love. Paul prays that it may abound, and that his friends may have ever richer and deeper experiences of this love of God present in human life.

The Christian life simply puts first values first. Paul's prayer concentrates on the highest of all values: that Christians' lives may simply be "to the glory and praise of God."

### 100. Hope Sustains Us in the Sufferings of Life

Rom 8, 24-25
Pentecost Vigil-b

In hope we were saved.
But hope is not hope if its object is seen;
how is it possible for one to hope for what he sees?
And hoping for what we cannot see
means awaiting it with patient endurance.

We are already justified by faith, and we look forward with hope to a final future salvation. We are already raised with Christ in Baptism, but it is hope that enables us to bear with the sufferings of the present. Hope makes the Christian a witness before the world of a lively faith in the resurrection.

Hope lives on trust of the beloved. Like faith, it is powerful enough to maintain a bridge across the darkness of this life. If everything were handed to us on a silver platter, our love would be without the opportunity to become mature. Maturity means making a choice in faith and trust, when another choice—in many ways more humanly attractive—is always clamoring for our attention.

## 101. All Creation Hopes for Redemption

Rom 8, 18-23
15A
Pentecost Vigil-a

I consider the sufferings of the present to be as nothing
compared with the glory to be revealed is us.
Indeed, the whole created world eagerly awaits the
    revelation of the sons of God.
Creation was made subject to futility, not of its own
    accord
but by him who once subjected it;
yet not without hope, because the world itself will be
    freed
from its slavery to corruption
and share in the glorious freedom of the children of
    God.
Yes, we know that all creation groans and is in agony
    even until now.
Not only that, but we ourselves,
although we have the Spirit as first fruits,
groan inwardly while we await the redemption of our
    bodies.


Paul paints two pictures of the world—one of sickness,
pain and sin; the other of greatness and hope, strength
and joy. The sick one hides the hopeful one; the sufferings of today hide the glory of God's day as the earth
hides a seed.

In one picture the earth is a huge, stupid mess,
purposeless and frustrated; not through its own fault,
but because of what man has done. In the other, this
"slave" world is transformed by changing masters, by
becoming a "child" of God. Instead of serving rotten-
ness and death the world will come to bloom, free as
a flower.

The deep hope that is fixed in both man and nature
is a sign that God will glorify both. We Christians are a
beginning for all the rest of creation because we already
have something new—a fresh breath from Jesus, a spring

wind, his Holy Spirit already at work in our bodies. It is
necessary to keep in mind the double meaning of
*pneuma*—"spirit." It means the Third Person of the
Trinity as well as the air we breathe. The work of the
Spirit, the fresh air, is a starting point for the liberation
of all creation.

Paul does not spell out what glorification will bring to
irrational creation. But, just as man's sin involved all
creation, so will his glorification.

## G.  CHARITY

### 102.  God's Greatest Gift Is Love

1 Cor 12, 31–13, 13
4C

Set your hearts on the greater gifts.
Now I will show you the way which surpasses all the
     others.
If I speak with human tongues and angelic as well,
but do not have love,
I am a noisy gong, a clanging cymbal.
If I have the gift of prophecy
and, with full knowledge, comprehend all mysteries,
if I have faith great enough to move mountains,
but have not love, I am nothing.
If I give everything I have to feed the poor
and hand over my body to be burned,
but have not love, I gain nothing.
Love is patient; love is kind.
Love is not jealous,
it does not put on airs, it is not snobbish.
Love is never rude, it is not self-seeking,
it is not prone to anger; neither does it brood over

injuries.
Love does not rejoice in what is wrong
but rejoices with the truth.
There is no limit to love's forbearance,
to its trust, its hope, its power to endure.
Love never fails. Prophecies will cease,
tongues will be silent, knowledge will pass away.
Our knowledge is imperfect and our prophesying is
    imperfect.
When the perfect comes, the imperfect will pass away.
When I was a child I used to talk like a child,
think like a child, reason like a child.
When I became a man I put childish ways aside.
Now we see indistinctly, as in a mirror;
then we shall see face to face.
My knowledge is imperfect now;
then I shall know even as I am known.
There are in the end three things that last:
faith, hope, and love,
and the greatest of these is love.

The highest kind of love is *agape*, God's own kind of love, made visible in Jesus. Its motive is totally unselfish: No personal benefit is sought or even contemplated. It does not have to be attracted by the goodness of the beloved; it seeks nothing, wants nothing but the good of the beloved. This love is best seen in God's love for sinners. There is nothing naturally attractive about them—yet they are precious to God because he is simply Love, creating and healing.

This is the greatest gift God can give us. Paul here reminds the Corinthians of the immeasurable superiority of charity over particular charismatic gifts which they were overvaluing.

Even among these charismatic gifts it seems Paul first intended to counsel them to seek the "higher" ones. Then he was impelled to remind them of *the* greatest of all, the *way* of charity, the theological virtue that reaches directly to God. Without this charity the charismatic gifts are nothing: prayer (tongues), preaching (prophecy, knowledge) and action ("moving mountains," generosity, even death) are worthless.

Love patiently suffers injuries from the beloved (that is, one's neighbor, everyone). It renders steady service. It is content, and hence cannot be provoked to envy. It cannot put on airs, since it has no distorted self-concern or insecurity. It is tactful, considerate, respectful of others' rights, weaknesses and feelings. It is concerned about others' welfare, not its own. It is not given to vindictive or selfish anger and maintains peace and self-composure even when injured. It looks for what is good, discounts what is evil, and applauds virtue. It gives scope to the beloved's wishes and needs and accepts the idiosyncrasies that mark every person. No amount of imperfection in the beloved can destroy its steadfastness; all things are interpreted in as favorable a light as possible.

Love's forgiveness never ends; no pressure can weaken it, no betrayals can destroy it, no darkness can extinguish its hope.

Love will last forever, whereas the charismatic gifts, valuable as they are, are temporary. One day we will no longer use or need them just as we no longer use the toys of childhood.

In that perfect day, our love will come face to face with God. Now we know him indirectly. Paul's comparison is between seeing someone before us and seeing that person's blurred and darkened reflection in one of the imperfect mirrors of the time. I am already "known" (intimately united) by the love of God; when the day of heaven comes, I shall myself "know" God as clearly as I now love him. As my love is now, so will my face-to-face vision be.

So there are three virtues which *abide* in the Christian life—in contrast to charismatic gifts which do not abide but are *temporary*—faith, hope and charity. Strictly speaking, faith and hope no longer continue in heaven insofar as their object is the God not yet directly possessed; but they do remain as an *attitude* of fidelity and a spirit of childlike confidence. Yet the greatest and most abiding gift we will have forever is love, *agape*, which is the fountain and final form of all the others.

### 103. Love Underlies All Commandments

Rom 13, 8-10
23A

Owe no debt to anyone
except the debt that binds us to love one another.
He who loves his neighbor has fulfilled the law.
The commandments, "You shall not commit adultery;
you shall not murder;
you shall not steal;
you shall not covet,"
and any other commandment there may be
are all summed up in this,
"You shall love your neighbor as yourself."
Love never does any wrong to the neighbor,
hence love is the fulfillment of the law.

Love is not one commandment among many. It is called for by every commandment. Various obligations point out the external mode of fulfilling the general law of love. But this general law of love is an internal commitment directed to one's neighbor. It is interesting that Paul did not feel the need to mention love of God here, obviously because true love of neighbor expresses love of God.

The only obligation a Christian need feel is that which arises from the needs, failures, even wickedness of his neighbors. Paul presumes that his Christian readers are lovers. Those who actually love have taken care of the Law—that of Moses, with its countless stipulations, as well as any other directives to external conduct.

Any commandment, such as those mentioned from among the 10, really points to the deeper law which Jesus emphasized (Lv 19, 18; Mt 5, 43). The last line suggests that love just cannot cause harm because it is going in the same direction as law, and far beyond.

"The sum-total of Christian ethics is 'to love one another.' There is no duty that is not included in 'love,' and nobody that is not included in 'one another' " (T. W. Manson).

### 104. Charity Imitates the Father and Jesus and Pleases the Spirit

Eph 4, 30–5, 2
19B

Do nothing to sadden the Holy Spirit
with whom you were sealed against the day of
    redemption.
Get rid of all bitterness, all passion and anger,
harsh words, slander, and malice of every kind.
In place of these, be kind to one another,
compassionate, and mutually forgiving,
just as God has forgiven you in Christ.
Be imitators of God as his dear children.
Follow the way of love, even as Christ loved you.
He gave himself for us as an offering to God,
a gift of pleasing fragrance.

Unkindness is disrespect for the Spirit who lives in people of faith. In Baptism Christians are sealed with the Spirit in preparation for the final day of redemption when they will be branded as belonging to God (cf. the "mark of the Lamb" in Revelations). Charity is called for by the Spirit within us; it is not merely an imposed law.

The other side of the coin of charity is forgiveness. This is much more than not taking revenge. It is a positive, generous act of love in imitation of the Father and Jesus. For we should be children of God by imitation, not only by our being.

We are his "dear" children. The Greeks emphasized this aspect. Loving children imitate their fathers.

We are also imitators of Christ. His generous sacrifice of himself was, in the Old Testament sense, something fragrant that ascended to the Father. Fragrance marks the sacrificial change from inert granules (e.g., of incense) to a pleasing aroma. We join our sacrifice to Christ's; his fragrance graces our own love and forgiveness.

### 105. Charity Is All Things to All Men

1 Cor 9, 19-23
5B-b

Although I am not bound to anyone
I made myself the slave of all
so as to win over as many as possible.
To the weak I became a weak person
with a view to winning the weak.
I have made myself all things to all men
in order to save at least some of them.
In fact, I do all that I do for the sake of the gospel
in the hope of having a share in its blessings.

Charity often means simply adapting to other people. Paul has been appealing to certain broad-minded people in Corinth to be careful not to scandalize others by eating meat offered to idols. They have a right to eat the meat, but they have no right to scandalize anyone. Paul himself has given up many things to which he has a right as an apostle. For instance, he has refused to accept any

131

wages for his services in preaching the gospel.

Far from asserting his rights, he has adapted himself to everyone. He has respected Jewish belief as much as possible; he has adapted his teaching to the Gentiles who knew nothing of Jewish traditions; he has made concessions to the "weak" who do not yet fully understand their Christianity, as in the case of those who are worried about meat offered to idols.

As long as principle is not involved, he will defer to anyone's need "to save at least some of them"—a phrase that seems to betray some sadness at the meager results he has had. Yet, as long as the Lord wants him on earth, he will be the slave of all.

## 106. Accepting One Another for God's Glory

Rom 15, 4-9
2 Advent A

Everything written before our time
was written for our instruction,
that we might derive hope from the lessons of patience
and the words of encouragement in the Scriptures.
May God, the source of all patience and encouragement,
enable you to live in perfect harmony with one another
according to the spirit of Christ Jesus,
so that with one heart and voice you may glorify God,
the Father of our Lord Jesus Christ.
Accept one another, then, as Christ accepted you
for the glory of God.
Yes, I affirm that Christ became the servant of the Jews
because of God's faithfulness
in fulfilling the promises to the patriarchs
whereas the Gentiles glorify God because of his mercy.
As Scripture has it, "Therefore I will praise you among
the Gentiles
and I will sing to your name."

The context of this passage is Paul's appeal for brotherhood—for "acceptance"—between "weak" and "strong," between strictly observant Jews and "free" Gentiles. Paul stresses the help God gives us in the Hebrew Scriptures: They show us lessons of patience and give us hope and encouragement in our difficulty in accepting others.

They and we are to accept one another as Jesus accepted us and as God accepted us in Jesus. He accepted the Jews—became their servant—because of God's faithfulness to his promises to the Chosen People. He accepted the Gentiles simply out of mercy. It was an acceptance of "difficult" persons in either case. Now God gives us his own Spirit so that we may accept one another and fulfill our first purpose—to glorify him in Christ.

### 107. Charity Does Not Look on Others in a Merely Human Way

2 Cor 5, 14-17
12B

The love of Christ impels us
who have reached the conviction
that since one died for all, all died.
He died for all so that those who live
might live no longer for themselves,
but for him who for their sakes died and was raised up.
Because of this we no longer look on anyone
in terms of mere human judgment.
If at one time we so regarded Christ,
we no longer know him by this standard.
This means that if anyone is in Christ,
he is a new creation.
The old order has passed away; now all is new!

There was a time when Paul thought of Christ (and, consequently all human beings) in a purely human way: Christ was a pretender to Messianic power, a condemned criminal and, in any case, a failure. There is no way of knowing whether Paul ever saw Christ before his death and resurrection. But after the experience on the road to Damascus, Paul sees everything and everyone in a new light—because all things *are* new.

He knows now that the one man, Christ, died as the representative of the whole human race and rose to a glorious new life. He shares this new life with all who accept it so they may lead new lives free of selfishness. Now Paul knows and loves and is united to this risen Christ; Christ's love in him possesses and controls him and produces his response of love.

Now he no longer looks on *anyone* in merely human terms. He sees all mankind as redeemed by the blood of Christ, precious to God, destined to receive eternal life.

### 108. All Social Stigmas Give Way
### Before the Brotherhood of Christians

Phlm 9-10. 12-17
23C

I, Paul, ambassador of Christ and now a prisoner for him,
appeal to you for my child,
whom I have begotten during my imprisonment.
It is he I am sending to you—
and that means I am sending my heart!
I had wanted to keep him with me,
that he might serve me in your place
while I am in prison for the gospel;
but I did not want to do anything without your consent,
that kindness might not be forced on you but freely
    bestowed.

Perhaps he was separated from you for a while for this
      reason:
that you might possess him forever,
no longer as a slave but as more than a slave,
a beloved brother, especially dear to me;
and how much more than a brother to you,
since now you will know him both as a man and in the
      Lord.
If then you regard me as a partner,
welcome him as you would me.

    Onesimus, a slave, had run away from Philemon,
probably taking some "supplies" with him. In Rome,
the runaway became a convert to Christianity through
the ministry of Paul, then in prison. Acceding to the
social structure of the day, Paul sends him back to his
rightful owner. He does not assert his authority, but
begs Philemon to welcome the slave as his new brother
in Christ.

    Paul could not change the social structure. It would
take centuries for Christian doctrine to permeate even a
part of society. But Paul lays down principles which
ultimately would make slavery impossible:  The slave is
the "master's" brother, both naturally and by grace.
Their friendship is eternal. No man can "own" another
man. Master and slave are equal—especially as servants
of the gospel.

    Paul exerts a little "pressure" on Philemon. He hints
that he really could have kept Onesimus with himself;
but he asks only that the slave be welcomed as a
"brother" (perhaps forgiven his offense of stealing?).
Philemon might even want to send him back to help
Paul. In any case, the slave deserves the same treatment
Paul would get from his friend.

## 109. Freedom Is for Serving Others

Gal 5, 1. 13-18
13C

It was for liberty that Christ freed us.
So stand firm, and do not take on yourselves
the yoke of slavery a second time!
My brothers, remember that you have been called
to live in freedom—
but not a freedom that gives free rein to the flesh.
Out of love, place yourselves at one another's service.
The whole law has found its fulfillment
in this one saying:
"You shall love your neighbor as yourself."
If you go on biting and tearing one another to pieces,
take care!
You will end up in mutual destruction!
My point is that you should live in accord with the
     spirit
and you will not yield to the cravings of the flesh.
The flesh lusts against the spirit and the spirit against
     the flesh;
the two are directly opposed.
This is why you do not do what your will intends.
If you are guided by the spirit,
you are not under the law.

Against those who would continue circumcision as a requirement of the Law (or any observance of Old Testament regulations), Paul insists that Christ has freed us to be really free. Christians must not return to any kind of moral slavery.

On the other hand, Paul is not anti-law. The Gentiles might easily have misunderstood, since they (unlike Jews) saw no great connection between religion and morality. "Raw" anarchic freedom, Paul says, will destroy the community. We are freed from legalism but not from responsibility.

Real freedom is freedom *for* serving others. The whole Law is summed up in love of neighbor. Real freedom has its source in the Holy Spirit, who is our indwelling principle and power. The Christian is no longer faced with *mere* law—demanding obedience but not giving the power to obey. The Spirit gives the power which the Law could not give.

Even though united to Christ, the Christian must still struggle against the "flesh"—the desire to be independent, to save himself by his own efforts. "Fleshly" legalists try to please God on their own, without the Spirit, and are forever frustrated. Christians let the Spirit control their actions and produce fruit in freedom.

### 110. Christian Churches Should Aid Each Other Materially

2 Cor 8, 7. 9. 13-15
13B

Just as you are rich in every respect
in faith and discourse, in knowledge,
in total concern,
and in our love for you,
you may also abound in your work of charity.
You are well acquainted with the favor
shown you by our Lord Jesus Christ:
how for your sake he made himself poor
though he was rich,
so that you might become rich by his poverty.
The relief of others ought not to impoverish you;
there should be a certain equality.
Your plenty at the present time should supply their
        need
so that their surplus may in turn one day supply your
        need,
with equality as the result.
It is written, "He who gathered much had no excess
and he who gathered little had no lack."

Paul is asking the Corinthian Church to send material aid to the poor mother-Church in Jerusalem. The Churches in Macedonia had been especially generous in their gifts for the poorer Christian Churches. The Church at Corinth is now asked to emulate them.

They have been blessed by God with many gifts of a spiritual nature. If they show charity to the poor, it will be a sign of one more spiritual gift they have.

The supreme motive for their charity should be the love that Jesus Christ showed for us. He made himself poor by becoming man, thereby enriching Christians through his saving life, death and resurrection.

An added motive is given by the thought that the Corinthians will in turn be enriched by the "surplus" of the poor Jerusalem community, that is, by the spiritual riches they share with the whole Church.

## H. PRAYER

### 111. The Spirit Prays Within Our Prayer

Rom 8, 26-27
16A
Pentecost Vigil-c

The Spirit too helps us in our weakness,
for we do not know how to pray as we ought;
but the Spirit himself makes intercession for us
with groanings which cannot be expressed in speech.
He who searches hearts knows what the Spirit means,
for the Spirit intercedes for the saints
as God himself wills.

Paul is assuring his readers that the sufferings of this world are nothing in comparison to the glorification

that will come to us. There is an *assured* glory that
awaits us in the kingdom. We have certain hope of this.
Besides, we have the Spirit, which helps us pray as we
should for this glorification.

We are naturally weak. We do not know very much
about the "what" of our prayer, that is, our final glorification. But the Spirit intercedes "over and beyond"
us. All prayer, of course, is the work of the Spirit. It is
by the Spirit that we are able to say "Abba!" (Rom 8,
15; Gal 4, 6). More important than any words we say is
the Spirit through whom we say them. God looks
beyond the words, beyond our success or failure with
words or thoughts. He judges hearts, not externals; he
sees our growing integrity which shows that we welcome
his Spirit.

Specifically Paul seems to be saying that believers,
beyond the essential help of the Spirit for any prayer,
experience feelings they cannot put into words. He may
be referring to the intensity of prayer, even ecstatic
prayer. These wordless utterances are the language of
the Spirit, obviously most understandable by God.
"When our prayer gropes and falters, this Spirit inspires
charismatic urges deep in the soul, which are powerful
before God" (Barnabas Ahern, C.P.).

## 112. Confidence In God

2 Thes 2, 16– 3, 5
32C

May our Lord Jesus Christ himself,
may God our Father who loved us and in his mercy
        gave us eternal consolation and hope,
console your hearts and strengthen them
for every good work and word.
For the rest, brothers, pray for us

that the word of the Lord may make progress
and be hailed by many others, even as it has been
    by you.
Pray that we may be delivered from confused and
    evil men.
For not everyone has faith;
the Lord, however, keeps faith;
he it is who will strengthen you and guard you against
    the evil one.
In the Lord we are confident that you are doing
and will continue to do whatever we enjoin.
May the Lord rule your hearts in the love of God
and the constancy of Christ.

A great concern of our prayer should be that the
word of God may penetrate the hearts of people. This
is the work of God's grace, and Christians are always to
be intent on the saving act of God that fills human life.

Paul also asks for prayers for delivery from confused
and evil men—possibly his own persecutors, or the ones
leading people to believe that the *parousia* is imminent.

At the heart of all prayer is the certainty that God is
faithful in protecting us against evil and the Evil One.
The Christian life is to be ruled by the principle of love—
love from God, love for God.

The author begins his own prayer with a great
consciousness of what God has given—love, mercy,
consolation, hope. These gifts are the source of our
confidence for the future.

### 113.  Instructions on Prayer

1 Tm 2, 1-8
25C

First of all, I urge that petitions, prayers, intercessions,
    and thanksgivings be offered for all men,

especially for kings and those in authority,
that we may be able to lead undisturbed and tranquil
      lives
in perfect piety and dignity.
Prayer of this kind is good,
and God our savior is pleased with it
for he wants all men to be saved
and come to know the truth.
And the truth is this: "God is one.
One also is the mediator between God and men,
the man Christ Jesus,
who gave himself as a ransom for all."
This truth was attested at the fitting time.
I have been made its herald and apostle
(believe me, I am not lying but speak the truth),
the teacher of the nations in the true faith.
It is my wish, then, that in every place
the men shall offer prayers with blameless hands held
      aloft,
and be free from anger and dissension.

Paul is concerned that Timothy's people pray well together. Prayer should be offered for all men, because this joins us to God's desire to save all men and because our prayer pleases him.

In particular, we are to pray for civil authorities, instead of worshiping them as was done in the pagan cults. In contrast to the gods of these cults, there is but one saving God and one savior, Jesus. There is absolute certainty about this truth, of which Paul is the herald.

All prayer rests on the fact of Christ's ransoming us from sin. The literal meaning of ransom should not be emphasized: the duty of the next of kin to buy back land which his relative had been forced to sell. The important truth is our *kinship* with Christ, and the resulting privilege and duty of prayer.

Men (here meaning males—women are addressed in the following verses) should pray with hands that are dedicated to God, free of resentment and actual arguments. To pray with "hands held aloft" means to pray

with palms open and upward in expectation of God's
gifts.

## 114.  Prayer of Gratitude

Phil 4, 6-9
27A

Dismiss all anxiety from your minds.
Present your needs to God in every form of prayer
and in petitions full of gratitude.
Then God's own peace, which is beyond all
        understanding,
will stand guard over your hearts and minds,
in Christ Jesus.
Finally, my brothers, your thoughts should be wholly
        directed to all that is true,
all that deserves respect, all that is honest, pure,
admirable, decent, virtuous, or worthy of praise.
Live according to what you have learned and accepted,
what you have heard me say and seen me do.
Then will the God of peace be with you.

The universal remedy for all man's needs is grateful
prayer; we eliminate anxiety by entrusting our troubles
to God. Then peace—personified as a sentry—stands
guard over our minds and hearts and wards off confu-
sion and disturbance.

The second half of this reading is a statement of Christian humanism:  a list borrowed not from the Old Testament but from current Greek ways of thought. Paul
recommends the ideal natural virtues, "an epitome of
the charming aspects of the good life":  all that is true,
worthy of respect, well-ordered (just), pure, admirable,
decent. All virtue and praiseworthy conduct can be the
dwelling place of God's Spirit.

# I. MARRIAGE AND CELIBACY

## 115. Christian Marriage Symbolizes
## the Love of Christ and His Church

Eph 5, 21-32
21B

Defer to one another out of reverence for Christ.
Wives should be submissive to their husbands
as if to the Lord
because the husband is head of his wife
just as Christ is head of his body, the church,
as well as its savior.
As the church submits to Christ,
so wives should submit to their husbands in everything.
Husbands, love your wives, as Christ loved the church.
He gave himself up for her to make her holy,
purifying her in the bath of water by the power of
    the word,
to present to himself a glorious church,
holy and immaculate, without stain or wrinkle or
    anything of that sort.
Husbands should love their wives as they do their
    own bodies.
He who loves his wife loves himself.
Observe that no one ever hates his own flesh;
no, he nourishes it and takes care of it
as Christ cares for the church—
for we are members of his body.
"For this reason a man shall leave his father and
    mother,
and shall cling to his wife,
and the two shall be made into one."

This is a great foreshadowing;
I mean that it refers to Christ and the church.

Christ's life, death and resurrection has affected every institution including marriage. His self-sacrificing love is the model for home life. Husbands and wives show his presence and power by their mutual love and respect.

The first verse states the ideal of *all* Christian life—mutual deference out of reverence for Christ. Paul's words to wives, then, are but one particular example of the general mutual subjection within the Church.

It is true that, in the culture of the time, husbands were considered "superior" to wives. Paul uses this fact to make his comparison of husbands with Christ. Just as all Christians are to "follow the way of love, even as Christ loved you" (5, 2), so husbands are to love their wives with a similar sacrificial love.

The great "mystery" is God's long hidden secret, the plan to save the world in Christ. This mystery was foreshadowed in the institution of marriage as described in Genesis. The inmost and original meaning of marriage is its reflection of the love of Christ and his Church. It is not that the latter is "something like" marriage; rather, marriage is "something like" the union of Christ and his Body. The one parallels and illumines the other.

In Jewish marriages there was an interval between the making of the contract and the presentation of the bride. Perhaps our present life on earth is that interval. During this time the Church, called the Bride of the Lamb in the Book of Revelation, is being purified—a reference to the ritual bathing of the bride before marriage—so that Christ may have a perfect spouse.

All Christian morality is centered on the love and forgiveness Christ showed us. He is the model for both husbands and wives.

## 116. The Christian Family
## Is the Concrete Expression of the Church

Col 3, 12-21
Holy Family

Because you are God's chosen ones, holy and beloved,
clothe yourselves with heartfelt mercy,
with kindness, humility, meekness, and patience.
Bear with one another; forgive whatever grievances you
      have against one another.
Forgive as the Lord has forgiven you.
Over all these virtues put on love,
which binds the rest together and makes them perfect.
Christ's peace must reign in your hearts,
since as members of the one body you have been called
      to that peace.
Dedicate yourselves to thankfulness.
Let the word of Christ, rich as it is, dwell in you.
In wisdom made perfect, instruct and admonish one
      another.
Sing gratefully to God from your hearts in psalms,
      hymns, and inspired songs.
Whatever you do, whether in speech or in action,
do it in the name of the Lord Jesus.
Give thanks to God the Father through him.
You who are wives, be submissive to your husbands.
This is your duty in the Lord.
Husbands, love your wives.
Avoid any bitterness toward them.
You children, obey your parents in everything
as the acceptable way in the Lord.
And fathers, do not nag your children
lest they lose heart.

Christ has formed a new community. Therefore a
new spirit must appear in Christian relationships. In
particular the Christian family, the "domestic church,"
is the concrete expression of the Church's community.

From the new inner spirit come compassion, kindness,
humility, meekness, patience—in contrast to (3, 8) anger,
temper, malice, insults, foul language. The virtues, except

for "lowliness," or humility, are common even on the pagan lists of the time. The difference is Christ. His love is the unifying element in all virtues, covering them all like a garment—the "uniform" that identifies the Christian.

The motivation for Christian conduct lies in the fact that the Church is God's Chosen People—chosen, holy, beloved. This is God's endearing term for his people in the Old Testament.

Christ's peace (shalom, total well-being) is his reconciling of all persons and all things. This peace is like an umpire that decides between conflicting interests. The presence of Christ will be evident by the wisdom and gratitude of Christians' words and songs.

The family takes its holiness from its membership in the Body, at the same time it forms that Body in its role as the "little church." While preserving the concept of authority, the table of household duties stresses the fact that obligations are mutual—"each other" is said five times.

Wives are to be submissive *in the Lord*. It is not only children who have duties, but parents also. The Christian education of children must not be so demanding as to discourage them.

### 117. Celibacy as an Enabling Way of Life

1 Cor 7, 32-35
4B

I should like you to be free of all worries.
The unmarried man is busy with the Lord's affairs,
concerned with pleasing the Lord;
but the married man is busy with this world's demands
and is occupied with pleasing his wife.
This means he is divided.

The virgin—indeed, any unmarried woman—
is concerned with things of the Lord,
in pursuit of holiness in body and spirit.
The married woman, on the other hand,
has the cares of this world to absorb her
and is concerned with pleasing her husband.
I am going into this with you for your own good.
I have no desire to place restrictions on you,
but I do want to promote what is good,
what will help you to devote yourselves entirely to
    the Lord.

Whether or not Paul thought the *parousia* was imminent, he did give us some reasons why celibacy is always one important witness in the Church. Celibacy sets up a new and unique relationship between the celibate and the Christian community—an *enabling* one. It enables him or her to do some things which the concerns and cares of married persons cannot permit them to do.

Celibacy for the kingdom, it seems, existed in a different atmosphere than it does today, when so much emphasis is put on romantic love. Marriage for the ancients was a very important role, but history seems to indicate that it may have had little or nothing to do with love, vocation, personal commitment, etc. It amounted to a job. It was arranged, rather than chosen. Hence, from a pragmatic human viewpoint, marriage was something not to get into, a tying-down thing, a caring for things and a pleasing of one's spouse that was not necessarily connected with love. Marriage was one thing, love another, and so the man was divided, and the woman too.

## 118.  Chastity for All Christians

1 Cor 6, 13-15. 17-20
2B

The body is not for immorality;
it is for the Lord, and the Lord is for the body.
God, who raised up the Lord,
    will raise us also by his power.
Do you not see that your bodies are members of Christ?
Whoever is joined to the Lord becomes one spirit with
    him.
Shun lewd conduct.
Every other sin a man commits is outside his body,
but the fornicator sins against his own body.
You must know that your body is a temple of the
    Holy Spirit,
who is within—the Spirit you have received from God.
You are not your own.
You have been purchased, and at what a price!
So glorify God in your body.

Paul is showing the evil of sexual sins against those
who were using "liberty" as an excuse, saying that
sexual gratification was simply satisfying a natural
appetite, and was as permissible as eating and drinking.
Pagans felt that fornication was acceptable if there was
no force or fraud.

Christians base chastity on faith-Baptism. We are
members of Christ in our *bodies*, not just in a "spiritual"
way. Sexual nature belongs to Christ as well as the rest
of our physical nature. Each of us, embodied spirits and
enspirited bodies, is a member of Christ's Body. We are
*physically* united to Christ, this being best seen in the
Eucharist and the other sacraments.

The union of bodies in fornication is a mockery of
this physical union with Christ, just as the physical
union of Christian marriage symbolizes Christ's union
with his Bride the Church. The Church is made up of
*body*-persons.

By his death, Christ acquired a right to us, and in

faith-Baptism we agree. A Christian has no right to give the body away.

Having illicit relations affects a person's whole personality. The sex relationship is a handing over of oneself into the power of another. It is not an isolated, transient thing, but one that unites man and woman in an intimate, complete and enduring bond.

The Holy Spirit consecrates our body now, and will give us a share in Christ's glorious resurrection. We will become the "spiritual bodies" of the resurrection, but remain body-spirits in some form.

## J. PROCLAIMING THE GOOD NEWS

### 119. We Have No Choice
### But to Proclaim the Good News

1 Cor 9, 16-18
5B-a

Preaching the gospel is not the subject of a boast;
I am under compulsion and have no choice.
I am ruined if I do not preach it!
If I do it willingly, I have my recompense;
if unwillingly, I am nonetheless entrusted with a charge.
And this recompense of mine?
It is simply this,
that when preaching I offer the gospel free of charge
and do not make full use of the authority the gospel
     gives me.

Paul has renounced any recompense for his services, and lest his people think he is preparing to ask for something, he says he would rather die than change the practice.

Actually, preaching the gospel is not something for which he could take credit of any kind. The power of God works through the gospel itself; Paul is merely an instrument. He really has no choice about preaching the gospel; the grace of Christ "forces" him. He is like a slave that does the master's bidding without any thought of recompense. His only reward is in receiving no reward, so that he can be sure there are no personal, selfish "angles" in his work.

## 120.  Apostolic Proclamation of the Good News

2 Cor 4, 13-15
10B-a

We have that spirit of faith of which the Scripture says,
"Because I believed, I spoke out."
We believe and so we speak,
knowing that he who raised up the Lord Jesus
will raise us up along with Jesus
and place both us and you in his presence.
Indeed, everything is ordered to your benefit,
so that the grace bestowed in abundance may bring
      greater glory to God,
because they who give thanks are many.

The inner conviction of faith is the cause of our fearless speaking out for the faith, our proclaiming the Good News. There is a natural desire to share what we value.

This faith is inextricably joined to hope—our absolute conviction that God will raise us up and bring us, all together, into his presence. It is all one simple, beautiful plan:  Everything the apostle and minister Paul does is for Christians' benefit, for the sake of their salvation; and their salvation is to have the privilege of giving glory to God.

## 121. Proclaiming the Good News Entails Hardship

2 Tm 1, 6-8. 13-14
27C

I remind you to stir into flame the gift of God
bestowed when my hands were laid on you.
The Spirit God has given us is no cowardly spirit,
but rather one that makes us strong, loving and wise.
Therefore, never be ashamed of your testimony to our
    Lord,
nor of me, a prisoner for his sake;
but with the strength which comes from God
bear your share of the hardship which the gospel
    entails.
Take as a model of sound teaching
what you have heard me say,
in faith and love in Christ Jesus.
Guard the rich deposit of faith
with the help of the Holy Spirit who dwells within us.

Timothy was a convert of Paul's and his fellow
apostle for 15 years. Paul urges him to overcome his
timidity and hesitation and to stir up into flame the
gift he received by ordination at Paul's hands. He must
expect to suffer as Paul (now in prison) does for preaching the faith.

Timothy is to teach what he has learned from Paul:
not a mere message, but a proclamation of faith and
love—a dependable word, sound teaching.

Helped by the Holy Spirit, he is to guard the rich
deposit ("the good trust") of faith—the total revelation
made by Christ.

## 122. Paul, the Authentic Apostle

Gal 1, 11-19
10C

I assure you, brothers, the gospel I proclaimed to you
is no mere human invention.
I did not receive it from any man,
nor was I schooled in it.
It came by revelation from Jesus Christ.
You have heard, I know,
the story of my former way of life in Judaism.
You know that I went to extremes
in persecuting the Church of God
and tried to destroy it;
I made progress in Jewish observances
far beyond most of my contemporaries,
in my excess of zeal
to live out all the traditions of my ancestors.
But the time came
when he who had set me apart before I was born
and called me by his favor
chose to reveal his Son through me,
that I might spread among the Gentiles
the good tidings concerning him.
Immediately, without seeking human advisers
or even going to Jerusalem to see those who were
       apostles before me,
I went off to Arabia; later I returned to Damascus.
Three years after that I went up to Jerusalem
to get to know Cephas, with whom I stayed fifteen days.
I did not meet any other apostles
except James, the brother of the Lord.

Some Christians who insisted on observing the whole
Jewish law had apparently accused Paul of getting his
message from other preachers, not from Christ, and of
having watered it down to gain Gentile converts. His
main purpose here is to assert the divine nature of his
call to apostleship. The Good News—that every person
can be saved in Christ—was revealed to him in his experi-

ence of Christ on the road to Damascus. He is independent of, but in agreement with, the other apostles.

Paul's personal background hardly pointed in this direction. He was a most observant Jew, scrupulously observing all the traditions the Pharisees had added to the Law, and he persecuted the new "people of God" (the same phrase used for the Chosen People in the Old Testament).

Indeed God has "set him apart" (Pharisee means "separated") before his birth for the vocation of being an apostle. After his experience on the road to Damascus, he spent three years, probably in prayer and reflection, before going to the central Church in Jerusalem. The experience on the road had illumined him about Christ and his meaning for all men—the essential heart of the gospel. He went to Jerusalem to get information from Peter about Jesus' life and ministry. (Phrases in Paul's letters show a form similar to other parts of the New Testament in recording the original preaching.) Paul is therefore one with the Twelve in apostleship— and his, like theirs, came directly from Christ.

### 123. Paul, the Selfless Missionary

1 Thes 2, 7-9. 13
31A

While we were among you we were as gentle
as any nursing mother fondling her little ones.
So well disposed were we toward you, in fact,
that we wanted to share with you not only God's
     tidings
but our very lives, you had become so dear to us.
You must recall, brothers, our efforts and our toil:
how we worked day and night
all the time we preached God's good tidings to you

in order not to impose on you in any way.
That is why we thank God constantly
that in receiving his message from us you took it,
not as the word of men, but as it truly is,
the word of God at work within you who believe.

Paul responds to various accusations about his apostleship and ministry.

He did not impose his authority or demand financial aid. Rather, he supported himself. Above all, he shared himself with his converts and showed them gentleness and affection.

Paul's selflessness and his single-minded concern for his converts enabled the word of God which he preached to shine forth in all its magnificence and power. It was in no way obscured by any self-serving designs on the part of the preacher.

# V. The End and the Beginning

## 124. Glory to God in the Highest!

Rom 11, 33-36
21A

How deep are the riches
and the wisdom
and the knowledge of God!
How inscrutable his judgments,
how unsearchable his ways!
For "who has known the mind of the Lord?
Or who has been his counselor?
Who has given him anything so as to deserve return?"
For from him
and through him
and for him
all things are.
To him be glory forever.
Amen.

This is Paul's hymn to the mystery of God's wisdom and graciousness. God's ways are beyond human ken. Paul is perhaps especially mindful of the governance of the universe hidden behind present suffering.

God alone has *doxa*, glory. Our questioning of God's ways collapses in the face of his creating and redeeming all things.

God wills to save all persons. His power, wisdom and mercy is not thwarted by sin or put into debt by man's good works. Giving man freedom, God achieves his purpose.

It is our nature and our grace to be totally in God's loving hands. The most fitting response we can make is Jesus' own reverence for the Father, endless gratitude for his graciousness, and the angels' eternal song:
Glory to God in the highest!

# Indexes

# Index of Sundays and Feasts

## (Listed according to chapter numbers.)

The letters A, B, C refer to the three-year cycle of readings. A single number refers to one of the "34 Sundays of the Year." For example, 14C means the 14th Sunday of the Year in the C cycle. Some Sunday readings are divided into several units.

**Advent Season**
1 Advent A, 92
1 Advent B, 47
1 Advent C, 98
Immaculate Conception, 1, 3
2 Advent A, 106
2 Advent C, 99
3 Advent B, 13
3 Advent C, 97
4 Advent A, 16
4 Advent B, 81

**Christmas Season**
Midnight Mass, 14
Dawn Mass, 66
Holy Family, 116
January 1, 70
2nd of Christmas, 1, 84
Epiphany, 40

**Lenten Season**
1 Lent A, 18
1 Lent C, 88
2 Lent A, 7
2 Lent B, 5
2 Lent C, 75
3 Lent A, 32
3 Lent B, 57
3 Lent C, 55

4 Lent A, 67
4 Lent B, 10
4 Lent C, 19
5 Lent A, 33
5 Lent C, 29
Passion Sunday, 15

**Easter Season**
Holy Thursday, 78
Easter Vigil, 65
Easter, 69, 71
Ascension, 24, 84
Pentecost Vigil, 101, 100, 110
Pentecost, 36

**Solemnities of the Lord**
Trinity A, 4
Trinity B, 31
Trinity C, 32
Corpus Christi A, 79
Corpus Christi C, 78

**Season of the Year**
2A, 39
2B, 118
2C, 37
3A, 48
3B, 94
3C, 43, 44

4A, 11
4B, 117
4C, 102
5A, 85
5B, 105, 119
5C, 22
6A, 90
6B, 82
6C, 74
7A, 49
7B, 26
7C, 73
8A, 50
8B, 38, 8
8C, 76
9A, 83
9B, 60
9C, 52
10A, 86
10B, 61, 120
10C, 122
11A, 20
11B, 89
11C, 87
12A, 18
12B, 107
12C, 45
13A, 65
13B, 110
13C, 109
14A, 33, 35
14B, 63
14C, 58
15A, 101
15B, 1, 2, 3
15C, 17
16A, 111
16B, 21
16C, 59
17A, 6
17B, 42

17C, 68
18A, 25
18B, 64
18C, 71
19A, 53
19B, 104
20A, 54
20B, 34
21A, 124
21B, 115
22A, 80
23A, 103
23C, 108
24A, 28
24C, 30
25A, 27
25C, 113
26A, 15, 46
26C, 72
27A, 114
27C, 121
28A, 12
28C, 56
29A, 91
29C, 51
30A, 41
30C, 62
31A, 123
31C, 95
32A, 77
32C, 112
33A, 93
33C, 96
34A, 23
34C, 9, 17
Assumption, 23

# Index of Scripture References

(Listed according to chapter numbers.)

**Romans**
1, 1-7, #16
3, 21-25.28, #83
4, 18-25, #86
5, 1-5, #32
5, 6-11, #20
5, 12-15.17-19, #18
6, 3-11, #65
8, 8-11, #33
8, 12-13, #35
8, 14-17, #31
8, 18-23, #101
8, 24-25, #100
8, 26-27, #111
8, 28-30, #6
8, 31-34, #5
8, 35.37-39, #25
9, 1-5, #53
10, 8-13, #88
11, 13-15.29-32, #54
11, 33-36, #124
12, 1-2, #80
13, 8-10, #103
13, 11-14, #92
14, 7-9, #28
15, 4-9, #106
16, 25-27, #81

**First Corinthians**
1, 1-3, #39
1, 3-9, #47
1, 10-13.17, #48
1, 22-25, #57
1, 26-31, #11
2, 1-5, #85
2, 6-10, #90

3, 16-23, #49
4, 1-5, #50
5, 6-8, #69
6, 13-15.17-20, #118
7, 29-31, #94
7, 32-35, #117
9, 16-18, #119
9, 19-23, #105
10, 1-6.10-12, #55
10, 16-17, #79
10, 31—11, 1, #82
11, 23-26, #78
12, 3-7.12-13, #36
12, 8-11, #37
12, 12-26, #43
12, 27-30, #44
12, 31—13, 13, #102
15, 1-11, #22
15, 12.16-20, #74
15, 20-26.28, #23
15, 45-49, #73
15, 54-58, #76

**Second Corinthians**
1, 18-22, #26
3, 1-3, #38
3, 4-6, #8
4, 6-11, #60
4, 13-15, #120
4, 13—5, 1, #61
5, 6-10, #89
5, 14-17, #107
5, 17-21, #19
8, 7.9.13-15, #110
12, 7-10, #63
13, 11-13, #4

**Galatians**
1, 1-2.6-10, #52
1, 11-19, #122
2, 16.19-21, #87
3, 26-29, #45
4, 4-7, #70
5, 1.13-18, #109
6, 14-18, #58

**Ephesians**
1, 3-6, #1
1, 7-10, #2
1, 11-14, #3
1, 15-18, #84
1, 20-23, #24
2, 4-10, #10
2, 13-18, #21
3, 2-3.5-6, #40
4, 1-6, #42
4, 17.20-24, #64
4, 30—5, 2, #104
5, 8-14, #67
5, 15-20, #34
5, 21-32, #115

**Philippians**
1, 4-6.8-11, #99
1, 20-24.27, #27
2, 1-5, #46
2, 6-11, #15
3, 8-14, #29
3, 17—4, 1, #75
4, 4-7, #97
4, 6-9, #114
4, 12-14.19-20, #12

**Colossians**
1, 12-14, #9
1, 15-20, #17
1, 24-28, #59
2, 12-14, #68

3, 1-5.9-11, #71
3, 12-21, #116

**First Thessalonians**
1, 1-5, #91
1, 5-10, #41
2, 7-9.13, #123
3, 12—4, 2, #98
4, 13-17, #77
5, 1-6, #93
5, 16-24, #13

**Second Thessalonians**
1, 11—2, 2, #95
2, 16—3, 5, #112
3, 7-12, #96

**First Timothy**
1, 12-17, #30
2, 1-8, #113
6, 11-16, #72

**Second Timothy**
1, 6-8.13-14, #121
1, 8-10, #7
2, 8-13, #56
3, 14—4, 2, #51
4, 6-8.16-18, #62

**Titus**
2, 11-14, #14
3, 4-7, #66

**Philemon**
9-10.12-17, #108

# Index of Topics

(Listed according to chapter numbers.)

Accepting others, 106
Adam, new, 14
Agape, 102
Aid, material, 110
Alertness, 93
Anxiety, 95
Apostle Paul, 122-123
Apostolate, 119-123
Apostolic authority, 52
Ascension, 24
Authority, 39, 50-52

Baptism, 56, 64-72
Blood, 78
Body of Christ, 36, 43
Body, our risen, 73-77
Brotherhood, 108

Call from God, 40
Celibacy, 94, 117
Charity, 48, 91, 102-110
Chastity, 118
Children of God, 31, 45
Chosen People, 55
Christ, 14-30
Christ crucified, 57
Christ's death, 65
Christ's suffering, 59
Christ's resurrection, 65
Christian life, 56ff
Church, 38-55
Church, evangelization, 41
Church and family, 116
Church, suffering, 59
Coming of Christ, 77, 92-101

Commandments, 103
Community, 4, 39, 41
Confidence, 5, 88, 112
Courage, 60
Covenant, first, 54-55
Covenant, new, 78
Creation, 101
Creation, new, 64
Cross, 56-58
Crucifixion with Christ, 56-63, 87

Death, Jesus' reconciling, 20
Death, baptismal, 56
Death, victory over, 76
Dependence, human, 10-11
Dissension, 47, 49
Disunity, 49
Divinity of Christ, 14, 16
Dying with Christ, 56ff

Enthronement, Jesus', 24
Eternal plan, 1-2
Eternal life, 61
Eucharist, 78-82

Factions, 47-49
Faith, 45, 83-91, 107
Faith, profession of, 72
Faithfulness, 26
Family, 115-118
"Flesh," 33-34
Forgiveness of God, 20, 68
Freedom, 45, 109
Fullness of time, 2

Gentiles, 40
Gift of faith, 83, 85-86, 91
Gifts of the Spirit, 36-37,
    43-44, 47
Glorification of Jesus, 24
Glory of God, 63, 81-82,
    106, 124
God's love, 5-6, 25, 32
God's will, 13
Grace, 14, 18-19, 63, 66
Gratitude, 114
Gratuitousness of grace,
    7, 9-11

Hardship, 121
Heaven, 61, 77
Holiness, 1, 11-12, 59,
    83, 86
Holiness, progress in, 98
Hope, 23, 32, 56, 58, 74,
    91, 92-101
Hour (*kairos*), 92
Humanity of Christ, 14,
    16, 70
Humanism, Christian, 114
Humility, 15, 46
Humility of Christ, 46

Institutional Church, 44
Incarnation, 14
Indwelling, 33
Israel, 53-55

Jesus, 2, 14-30
    ascension of, 24
    divinity of, 16
    emptying of, 15, 19
    enthronement of, 24
    faithfulness of, 26
    humanity of, 16
    incarnation of, 14

his love for us, 25
the new Adam, 18
as peacemaker, 21
primacy of, 17
resurrection of, 22-23
the sacrament of God,
    14
second coming of,
    92ff
union with, 27
Joy, 34, 97
Judgment, 88-89
Justification, 83, 86-87

Kairos, 92
Kerygma, 41

Law, 109
Liberation, 2, 71
Life, eternal, 61
Light, Jesus as the, 67
Love, 84, 102-110
Love from God, 5-6, 25,
    32

Marriage, 115-116
Mary, 70
Material aid, 110
Maturity, 90
Mercy of God, 10

Nearness of Christ, 97
New life in Baptism, 64,
    69, 71

Oneness of the Church, 42
Organization, Church, 44

Paul
    as example, 30
    suffering of, 62-63

as apostle, 122-123
Peace, 13, 97
Peacemaker, Jesus as, 21
Plan, eternal, 1
Poor, aid to, 110
Power from God, 12, 57, 60
Power of God, 63
Praise to God, 1
Prayer, 111-114
Preaching, 119-120
Present moment, 92
Proclaiming the Good News, 119-123
Progress, 93, 98
Public witness, 72
Purification, 64

Readiness, 93
Reconciliation, 20-21
Redemption of creation, 101
Response to God, 84, 91
Resurrection, Jesus', 22-24
Resurrection, our, 33, 71, 73-77
Resurrection, baptismal, 56
Risen bodies, 73
Risen Christ, 69, 74
Rising with Christ, 56ff, 65

Sacrament, Jesus as, 66
Sacrifice, 78-80
Salvation, 6, 13, 92
Scriptures and resurrection, 22
Second coming, 92ff
Service, 50-51, 109
Sin, 19, 35
Social stigmas, 108

Spirit, Holy, 3, 8, 13, 31-38, 42, 90, 111
Suffering, 56-63, 100, 121
Surrender to God, 28

Thanksgiving, 114
Transformation, 68, 75, 80
Trinity, 104

Union with Jesus, 27
Unity of Church, 36, 40, 42, 44-45, 48, 79
Urgency of Christ's coming, 41, 94

Values, 29, 99
Variety, 43

Waiting for Christ, 92ff
Will of God, 13
Wisdom, 57, 90
Work, 96
World, 64
Worship, 62